POWER TO CHOOSE explores the lives of those caught up in human conflict and tragedy, and the dynamics that caused them to triumph.

Among these inspiring stories of God's deliverance...

The shame of parental neglect and abuse:

Megan, harboring the shameful secret of sexual abuse and childhood neglect for years, finally sought counseling for debillitating depression. To her surprise, relief and joy, she finds deliverance and the healing of deeply painful memories.

The loss of a child without warning:

Barbara Dan writes of her experience: "When a control freak like myself suddenly realizes she has no control over the events of her life, it's a daunting experience. I had no control over what happened. I couldn't reverse the tragic fact of my baby's SIDS death. I couldn't deny it either. All I had left was a choice: How was I going to deal with my baby's death?"

The sorrow of watching a teenage son destroy his life through drugs and a life of crime:

Sandra Patterson, a minister's wife, faced a devastating test of her faith. "It was a living nightmare that held the entire family in its grip for nearly seven years," she recalls, looking back to a time when her teenage son, though a professed Christian, turned his back on his faith and became involved in drugs and a life of crime.

Read the story of her family's tears and private anguish, and ultimately how God used this family's tenacious love to work a miracle in their son's heart and life.

POWER
TO
CHOOSE

True Stories of Tragedy and Triumph

♦

**as told by Barbara Dan,
Sandra Patterson, and Family
Therapist John Dan, M.A., M.Div.**

EDEN PUBLISHING

8635 West Sahara Aveue, Suite 459
The Lakes, Nevada 89117

POWER TO CHOOSE

FIRST EDITION/Trade Paperback, ISBN 1-884898-07-6

Library of Congress Catalog Card Number 94-62200

EDEN PUBLISHING
8635 W. Sahara Avenue, Suite 459
The Lakes, Nevada 89117

◆

OTHER BOOKS BY JOHN DAN:
Power to Change
AND
Behold! The Lamb of God
(A Passover Seder Service for Christians)

◆

The personal accounts related in POWER TO CHOOSE are true. However, names, locations and certain details have been changed to preserve and protect the anonymity and right to privacy of those involved.

DEDICATION

To All Who Grieve, this book is dedicated with much love.

To Gudrun Babcock, a wise woman who, like Mary the mother of Jesus, "stored all these things in her heart," believing and trusting God in all things.

In loving memory of her son, David Milburn Babcock (1963-1994), a gifted follower of the Lord whose sudden death brightens heaven, making it even more a place of joyful expectation. Thank you, Lord, for sharing David with us. His joy in the Lord, his selfless sharing of himself, and his contagious faith continue to bear much fruit.

◆

To the families of murder victims: God knows who you are and holds you very close to His heart.

◆

And to you, the reader: Thanks for taking time to consider what God has laid on our hearts to share. It has been a joy—and a challenge—to portray faithfully what God is doing in the lives of so many. May you face each new day with a sense of expectation. God will not disappoint!

About the Authors...

Sandra Patterson and her husband Glenn now live in Southern California, where she owns her own insurance agency. In her spare time she tutors disadvantaged children part-time in an East Los Angeles community center. She enjoys writing poetry and doing needlepoint for relaxation, and frequently joins the rest of the family, including the five grandchildren, on camping trips throughout the western United States.

Barbara Dan has a diverse background, ranging from professional acting and television production to real estate, accounting, teaching, editing and publishing. She has a B.A. in Theatre Arts and an M.A. in Humanities. She has written a number of plays and novels, but considers raising four children her most challenging and rewarding career thus far.

John Dan has worked as a pastor, counselor and mental health clinician for the past thirty-two years. An ordained American Baptist minister, he has graduate degrees in Theology and Human Development Counseling. On staff at Southern Nevada Adult Mental Health Services for fourteen years, he directed Henderson Counseling Services for five of those years. Currently in private practice, he is a licensed Marriage and Family Therapist in California and Nevada and a clinical member of the American Association of Marriage and Family Therapists.

Other ministries include pastoring four churches, serving as chaplain for the Los Angeles County Jail system, and directing a Salvation Army alcoholic rehabilitation program. Married thirty-five years, he and his wife Barbara have four grown children and four grandsons.

Table of Contents

Section One. POWER TO CHOOSE

Power to Choose:

Whose Power Are We Really Talking About?

AND

What Are the Choices We Really Have?

by

John Dan, M.A., M.Div.

PREFACE

This book is not an invitation to speculation, philosophical debate, or religious theorizing. It is about *choice*. About living through crisis and pain.

It is written for the person who is in the throes of a potentially life-altering choice or crisis, and for those who stand at the crossroads of making a decision that may effect the way they deal with life from here on out. Or you may know someone who has been left stripped and defenseless by tragedy, and you want to understand more clearly what your friend is going through, and how to help.

This book contains example after example of men and women who have struggled with the same heartaches and heavy burdens you have, and they have *won!* We're not talking about mere survival here. We're talking about making wise decisions and choices that will not escalate or increase your pain. About allowing God to transform you and the experience (since you cannot escape it) into something more than bearable—*more* than tolerable. Much more, I think you will agree, as you begin to examine your options and find the power to overcome.

Dare I say it? **Power to Choose** is about discovery, about recognizing that you're on a great journey. A spiritual journey lived out in a physical body amidst many given tangibles and many more unseen but infinitely more vital issues which affect the human spirit.

Most of us view life as a lifespan, if we're lucky, of approximately three score ten point six years, starting with birth and ending with death. Our conception of time is filtered through those events and experiences we perceive with the physical senses. We are influenced, quite naturally, by what we see, hear, touch, smell, ingest, and so on. In other words, the data upon which we generally rely comes from the realm of feeling, or sensation, and the emotions. Even our belief systems and view of life tend to be shaped, in large part, by our experience of the physical world around us.

However, when we limit ourselves and our perceptions only to responding out of the limitations built into us as finite beings, we leave ourselves extremely vulnerable. This is particularly true when we are hit blind-side by tragedy, regardless of the form it takes. And please do not mistake my meaning, when I say that none of us can escape difficulties and sorrow. With all my heart I wish we could. But since we cannot avoid pain and suffering and loss, try as we may wish to, we need to consider our options.

To do that, we need to realize that we *do* have choices. Not so much about *what* has happened to complicate our pilgrimage here on earth, but about *how* we will deal with life in the here and now.

Most of us have either read Shakespeare's *Hamlet* or seen one of the many film versions. If we have, we may have asked ourselves how the drama would have played itself out, if Hamlet had not made such a "fatally flawed" choice. I am not referring to his famous soliloquy, "To be, or not to be," in which he toys with the idea of suicide, but with the *real* question, whether he should have listened to his father's "ghost" and gotten caught up in the evil and madness that raged all around him; for in doing so, he invited that same destructive spirit into his own heart, eventually bringing about even more death and destruction to everyone around him, and eventually to himself.

"Aye, that is the question:" **What do we believe and upon what do we base our choices?** *Hamlet* is but one of many classic cases in literature of the downward spiral created by getting caught up in what I describe as First Order thinking in my book, ***Power to Change***. All the great and enduring playwrights, from Aeschylus to Chekhov to Miller, have done a superlative job of portraying this destructive pattern within the human soul. Where they do *not* succeed is in showing us the way out of this trap, this pit of human despair.

The Holy Bible very clearly shows us the human condition. It minces no words about our alienation from God, our sinful knee-jerk reactions to life, our spiritual blundering, or our propensity to strike out in blind desperation.

Where the Bible differs from all other books on the face of the earth is in its clear message of hope. We *can* find our way through the maze of our pain and confusion and difficulty! God *has* made a "way of escape," not from the fire of our affliction, but from the fear that paralyzes and deadens and hinders our progress along life's journey.

This book will help you explore Biblical truths and the choices that are available to you, so that you may live, not amidst the carnage on the dung heap of Golgotha, from which Christ has come to rescue you, but on the Resurrection side of life's sorrows and trials.

But you will only do it...*by faith!*

It will not happen by relying on your own strength. This is not a do-it-yourselfer's manual, but a book about making healthy choices.

As a therapist for over thirty years, I will not lie to you: **No choice is healthy that does not place Christ at the absolute center of your life.** You cannot overcome and emerge victorious from the crucible of life's toughest experiences in your own strength. I have seen this proven out in countless lives, including my own and my family's. I have seen clients in the deepest pits of despair and loneliness and grief emerge into the radiant sunlight of a new day and a new life, solely through the exercise of the **power to choose...God.**

There is no other way.

I know that sounds dogmatic. Some may even accuse me of having a closed mind. I prefer to call it a "settled" mind. I know what works. As a trained clinical therapist and a Christian pastor, I have seen what people can do when they but choose the sovereignty of God.

More important, being flesh and blood, and as frail and vulnerable as you, I have been subject to the same trials and sorrows. I have found myself part of the human experiment, no different from any of my colleagues and contemporaries. In my pain, I have reached out and grasped at solutions the world offers and fails to deliver. *I have also tested the promises of God and never once found Him to fail.*

Having laid out my position clearly from the beginning, I will be outlining a number of choices we have that coincide and go along with the *essential* choice, which has to do with your relationship with God. But first, very briefly, because tragedy and pain tend to immobilize and impale us with a sense of hopelessness, here are a few questions we need to ask ourselves:

How am I going to deal with the immediate situation? In other words, find out what needs to be done immediately, and do it. Don't get ahead of yourself; just take care of the essentials—and that includes taking care of yourself. Avoid being judgmental; don't try to second-guess God. Rarely do you have all the facts in a situation upon sudden impact. Wait; do your homework before you act.

What is my response going to be? This question is a tough one, because it embraces the entire incident. If you or a loved one is the victim of someone else's negligent, malicious or deliberate actions, this is an extremely difficult question to answer. There are smaller issues here that you may be able to work through on your own, but I *strongly* suggest contacting legal counsel and a pastor or therapist who have the training necessary to help you work through the anger, sense of outrage, and other issues involved here.

How will my decisions effect others who are also hurting? It's hard, as the initial confusion and denial sets in, but you must realize that others have also been impacted by what has happened. Cultivate an awareness of what's going on around you. Don't set aside your own feelings or deny the truth of what happened. But remember: Isolating yourself from others who share your pain will only prolong it and may cause rifts and misunderstandings that can never be mended. Reach out to one another. Don't be afraid to show your grief. Be honest about your anger and bewilderment. Just don't dump on others. Later on, you will regret it, even if you're in the right. Bitterness never heals. And believe me, before you're finished, you will need all the healing you can get. It's available to you; just don't blow it.

Is there any way I can get beyond my own pain without bringing more destruction down on myself or others? In other words, can I stop the progression of destructive forces this event has set in motion?

The answer is **YES.**

Make a conscious choice not to let yourself and/or your loved ones slip into a victim mindset, as a result of harm already inflicted. Enough trauma has already occurred. The job of a hospital emergency triage, for instance, is to halt further damage from occurring. Bleeding must be stopped and repairs made to the injured victim, so that healing can take place. I realize this is a clumsy analogy and not a particularly attractive one. However, the walking wounded, including those without a visible scratch on them, are no less vulnerable and hurting than those who have suffered physical injury. Victimization goes *beyond* physical pain, inflicting an incalculable wound upon the human spirit. This requires immediate intervention, preferably before the survivors of a tragedy are even fully aware of the ramifications of what they now face.

Being close to and directly involved with the event, you may not be in a position to assess the situation objectively. Even if you think you are, you may wish to check out your perceptions with a qualified professional. In the long run, it's generally much more costly to undo mistakes than to seek help right away. If you see a destructive pattern of calamity and escalating pain start to develop, do not delay. Seek professional help right away.

Can I find meaning in the midst of this madness? That depends on you. It depends on the choices you make. Even if you've made a bad beginning in the grief process, it's not too late. You can choose to get out of the pit of despair and move on with your life. At any point on the merry-go-round of misery, you have the...**POWER TO CHOOSE.**

This book reflects a lifetime of ministering to those who have emerged from the crucible of life's harshest realities with a sense of certainty and victory. These are not stories without substance, but people who have overcome. I have yet to meet the person who is too far gone to tap into the unlimited resources of God in Christ. It's a matter of personal choice. It's an individual decision.

Each of us has to make up our own mind. **We all have the power to choose, and the choice to link up with God's power.** "Choose this day," the Bible urges. What have you got to lose? Oh, but you say, you've already lost everything. Not so, my friend. You have everything to gain by placing yourself in the strong, nail-pierced hands of Jesus.

The apostle Paul knew devastating loss, yet he wrote: "What things were gain to me, those I counted loss for ...the excellency of the knowledge of Christ Jesus my Lord: for whom I have suffered the loss of all things, and do count them but dung, that I may win Christ." [Philippians 3:7-8]

Paul refers to a mystery here, only revealed to those who have entered into the meaning of suffering. Pain is not something any of us welcome; let me make that perfectly clear. This is not a fellowship of masochists and victims, but of survivors who overcome whatever it is they face. "We are more than conquerors through Christ who loves us." [Romans 8:37]

My own family has undergone its share of trials and

heartaches. My counseling ministry spans over thirty years; I have witnessed and worked through every conceivable form of human misery imaginable. I have witnessed the heights and the depths of human despair, and felt it myself at times. My heart goes out to anyone who has stood beside a lonely grave, or sat helplessly by the hospital bed of an accident victim, or struggled day by day to raise a handicapped child, or dealt with any of a thousand other variations that involve human misery and pain.

Over time, I have come to recognize that, in many cases, **suffering opens up ministry to others**. Some experiences penetrate the soul so deeply that it's almost like hearing the cry of every other sorrowing parent; or getting inside the skin of every other person who has ever hurt. As we become sensitized to spiritual realities which supersede this physical realm, we find ourselves drawn in our helplessness into a fellowship of suffering that invariably leads us to the foot of the Cross, where Jesus Himself stands resplendent in the raiment of His power and majesty and Resurrection to welcome us. He of all men who have walked this earth understands our dilemma, our humanity, our deepest needs.

My friend, in His graciousness and love, God can and will get you through this moment, through the next hour and the next day. He will lead you through whatever lies ahead. You can trust Him completely and without reservation.

"Because [we] children are mere flesh and blood, Christ took on all the same vulnerabilities found in our humanity, so that by his death he might destroy him who holds the power of death--that is, the devil--and free those who all their lives were slaves to their fear of death...Having Himself suffered, He is able to sustain and uphold those who are tempted." [Hebrews 2:14-15, 18, paraphrased.]

God's role in our suffering may be difficult to grasp in the midst of your present circumstances and pain. But I can assure you, even in your darkest hour, you *can* experience victory and power. Out of the ashes of a razed forest will spring up a whole new life, stronger and better able to withstand the storms of life.

Let me encourage you to let the life stories in this book speak to your heart. These people share a lot in common with you and me, even though their way of handling life and what they have faced and overcome will probably not match your situation. Your response and your choices will be completely unique to your experience and to your spiritual, psychological and emotional make-up.

This book is not intended as a road-map to get you from Point X to Point Z. There are no shortcuts through the labyrinth of pain, believe me. But it is my prayer that these case histories will provide light for your path, as you step out with a degree more certainty to deal with your own heartache and pain.

It *is* possible to overcome evil with good. Life is about recapturing joy and meaning and purpose in the midst of overwhelming loss. This may seem a paradox to the average reader, but that's all right. *Power to Choose* has been written for those not so ordinary people whom God has lovingly chosen and empowered to bear His message of hope to the world. You may be one of them. You may not know it yet, but I think you will become aware of it, as you read on.

Know this from the outset: God loves you with an undying love. He did not single you out for misery or cause this to happen to you. But He *will* see you through, from start to finish. He only waits upon you.

So choose.

Let Him take the burden; let Him carry you.

He's right there, standing by your side. Waiting to shower you with His power and His love.

You are not alone.

Chapter 1. Power to Choose:
The Road to Mental and Spiritual Health

In the Genesis account of creation, the first couple were created in the trinitarian Image of God. As the capstone of God's glory, the man and the woman and their future offspring were intended to live in intimacy with their Creator in an environment of supreme joy and harmony. Their journey through life was to be traveled under His sovereign leadership, with the Creator empowering them to choose wisely and providing the resources each of us as a traveler needs to live. God entrusted them with the task of caretakers over the earth; they were to subdue, multiply, rule and have dominion over the rest of His creation.

The Creator also gave the first couple a stern warning not even to flirt with the knowledge of good and evil. The warning was issued out of love, for it was always His desire that those on life's journey should maintain an intimate relationship with Him. They would, He cautioned, lose their innocence the moment they became contaminated with the knowledge of good and evil.

There is no reason to rehash the outcome of this couple's decision, or to belabor the fact of their disobedience and the subsequent suffering they brought upon themselves. By not choosing to heed God's warning, the first couple bought the Big Lie, that seeking to be gods unto themselves would somehow be better than maintaining fellowship and a healthy dependence upon the integrity of God Himself. This choice alienated them and all future generations from God, who is the

Source of all life.

As a consequence, sin and unbelief entered the picture and distorted the human trinitarian Image. Since then, people have been traveling the many broad roadways of life, all oppressive, helter-skelter, full of turmoil and drudgery. The end result is that life, as we experience it, squeezes all the joy out of the human spirit, thereby inviting all the destructive forces that inevitably lead to death, on both the spiritual and physical level.

At this point, we need to realize the following:

1. All travelers on the broad way are impaired by a distorted Image of God.

2. Destructive, sinful, oppressive conditions are maintained and perpetuated by distorted beliefs, lies and deceptions.

3. Social rules and manipulative forces on the broad road are governed by a desire for power, control and conformity, all of which devalue the human spirit. This system fosters further alienation, demanding that love be earned or deserved, in direct opposition to God's original intent and ongoing mission, which is to reconcile us through His shed blood of the Cross and liberate us from the spirit of bondage.

4. Since this schism from God, social relationships have been adversarial in nature, dominated by hostility toward fellow travelers. On the broad way, travelers trudge on in a survival mode, alienated from God and other human beings.

5. Life on the broad roads of life is full of conflict, turmoil, bitterness and pain. The toll upon the human spirit is so great that the resultant misery does incalculable damage.

Jesus taught His followers that there are many broad roads leading to destruction and death, and that He alone is the narrow road that keeps people on track, empowering them to choose wisely. Through Him, life can be a creative growth process, joyous and productive, as long as we rely wholly upon His light and life within.

Few get a clear picture of what this narrow road entails. Misconceptions about the role and purpose of religion make people uneasy about traveling the narrow road. Because of disruptive inner voices, people tend to view any restraint or boundaries as an impediment to freedom.

Some grow discouraged, misinterpreting the teachings of Jesus as more legalistic, narrow-minded strictures upon the human spirit, when in actual fact His prescription for living leads to certainty and an absence of fear which in turn liberates. To these people's thinking, the narrow road seems to set parameters aimed at boxing them in. However, experience shows that it opens up a whole range of new possibilities, as those things which impede our spiritual progress are left by the wayside. It becomes part of the selection process.

Unless you have a clear and precise idea where you are going in life and what road to travel, your journey will resemble that of a junk peddlar, rather than the privileged child of the Kingdom that God intends you to be.

Jesus desires that we find and travel this narrow road in the full enjoyment and resources of Christ, who is the embodiment of Truth and the travelers' most steadfast Companion.

Since the first couple abandoned the narrow way to pursue their own willful way, generations have been marching the broad way to destruction. However, God in His gracious love and mercy sent His only begotten Son, Jesus, to take upon Himself our sinful nature, and thereby do away with the corruption and sin that distorts and interferes with the development of God's Image within us.

I describe this process in my book, *Power to Change,* as Christ absorbing our human condition, soaking up sin almost like a sponge, so that when He paid for our sins on the Cross, He "who knew no sin, became sin for us." [II Corinthians 5:21]

After absorbing all the vileness of our human condition, Christ imparts His life as an undeserved gift to those who will choose to receive His life and place themselves under His sovereign rule.

The narrow road now cuts across the broad open freeways of life, which promise everything and deliver little. The narrow road, by contrast, is a shining ribbon of light, illuminating the deadly human condition of sin that dominates this world.

It is mind boggling how tenaciously the human proclivity toward sin and alienation imbeds itself into the distorted trinitarian make-up of all broad way travelers. This condition impedes travelers from choosing Christ, who is the road of life.

For this reason, **it is essential that choice involve aligning ourselves with the sovereign will of God**. "Seek ye first the kingdom of God, and His righteousness, and all these things will be added unto you." [Matthew 6:33]

I must caution that there *are* choices that are simply unacceptable to God. We may desire His power for our lives, but access to God and His abundance are *only* available *on His terms.* We are His creation and cannot set the standard. This is simply not an option!

A couple of years ago on one of the national talk shows, a panel of homosexuals came on as guests to defend the so-called "gay" lifestyle. Among those expressing an opposing view were Sam and his wife Linda, both born-again Christians.

Sam was quite open about having been a practicing homosexual from an early age. In fact, he confessed that he had no problem at first with his sexual orientation. However, as time went on, he found himself becoming emptier and emptier. Finally he repented, surrendered his heart to Christ and was wonderfully converted.

Later, he met his future wife; he told her his history prior to their marriage. During the talk show, this couple stood up for their faith and took a strong stand against homosexuality (which, by the way, is rooted in self-preoccupation and denial).

Instantly two guests, a male and female, both claiming to be bisexual, began ardently to defend their lifestyle. In the process, this young couple were strongly criticized by the talk show host, other guests and members of the audience for being intolerant of homosexuals.

The homosexual guests took the stance that God loves them "as is," which is true, as far as the argument goes. But the argument was used to dodge the real issue, that God's love insists on transforming and delivering people from unnatural lifestyles, which are in His sight an "abomination."

The "gays" argued that they didn't want change, that it was necessary for others to accept and tolerate their behaviors, when in actual fact, their lifestyle is reprehensible. What they wanted was to maintain and remain in a sin-contaminated condition. They postured that love was manifested in their relationships. Both the male and female bisexuals did a lot of self-justification. They attacked the young couple as bigots; resenting, instead of recognizing the transformation that had taken place in Sam's life.

Their argument and contention are rather like Los Angeles gangster Mickey Cohen in the early fifties. Ludicrous as it sounds, he was outraged that he couldn't remain a "Christian" gangster. Gays, like heterosexual gangsters, nominal church-goers, etc., need to be saved and transformed into the trinitarian Image of God! This can only be accomplished when we submit ourselves to the sovereign will of God, thus allowing the Holy Spirit to bring about our inner transformation.

Those who have received **power to choose** the narrow road [God's way] have a clear view of what is healthy and act on it, *by choice*. By an act of their will, they choose health and wholeness. This requires movement; merely to maintain is to stagnate and die.

An example of static, unhealthy problem-solving can be found in the Pro-Choice Movement, a contradiction in terms, actually, since there *is* no movement, only two opposing forces in a no-win stand-off. Pro-Choice doesn't offer a choice, but represents a mindset that limits choice and discourages creative thought and action.

Today the ideas of Pro-Choice and Pro-Life have polarized into adversarial camps. In a healthy condition, one's adult-faith faculty is able to think, evaluate and choose. Pro-Choice gravitates toward indulgent and easy solutions, rather than seeking the power and grace of God to act responsibly and value life.

The philosophy behind a great many movements today, including pro-choice, thanatology, euthanasia, and other quick solution, "let somebody else take care of it" measures, is that if any other life interferes with ours, or becomes an inconvenience, we should be allowed to regard that life as expendable. If we doubt the heinous lengths to which some groups will go to carry out this nihilistic approach, we have only to recall the Holocaust and the millions of Jews and other hapless victims of the ovens and death camps across Europe. What is happening in Bosnia, Africa, Haiti, Russia, China, the United States—indeed, in every hemisphere of the earth, gives ample proof of man's continuing inhumanity toward his fellow man. (And this breakdown in basic human values includes both genders!)

The only way to stop these expressions of a deeply ingrained and sinister sickness within the human soul is for each of us, individually, to takes stock of our life and **choose** not to be a participant in such evil and darkness. We must look past the whitewash of distorted thinking that justifies our cruelty to one another. We must allow God to penetrate our darkness with His light and transforming love.

In my counseling ministry, one of the unhealthy expectations clients coming to me for the first time often have is the notion I will take over the decision-making process for them, that somehow I must, by virtue of my training, issue an edict from high that will relieve them of all responsibility for their actions and decisions. It is a very human failing for a client to tend toward transference, viewing the therapist as a parental or authority figure, a "rescuer." Any client evidencing such unrealistic views is soon shocked into reality by how quickly I dissuade them of such mistaken ideas!

The task of any reputable therapist, clergyman or politician is to empower people, not encourage dependency and magical thinking. This must be the purpose of government as well, not to foster dependence, which limits and narrows our options. Pipe dreams must be replaced by an objective examination of the facts.

One of the first things I do when a client comes to me is to strip away any false notions about my role as a therapist. Up front, I let them know two things:

1. I am not a miracle worker, and I am not into manipulation or mind-control. I offer no easy solutions. I want people to have the pleasure of charting their own destiny under the leadership of God. My role in their therapy is as a facilitator and encourager, not a guru.

2. I am not interested in providing people with a "quick fix," because magical solutions don't last, and in actual fact, are part of the delusional thinking that gets people in the muddle in which they find themselves.

What I attempt to do is encourage people to make intelligent choices that will move them into position, so that the full x-ray of God's transforming love can penetrate their thinking, help them examine their lives and all the evidence. Ultimately, I hope that the free exercise of their wills may bring "into captivity [their] every thought to the obedience of Christ"

[II Corinthians 10:5]. **For it is only when we choose the sovereignty of God in our lives that we experience true freedom and power for living.**

From the outset, I make it clear that each person's life journey is unique and that while I am perfectly willing to help them explore the journey thus far, including detours, alternate routes and deadends they may have encountered, the main purpose of our meeting is not to continue on the Superhighway of Life without a clue where they are or where they will wind up.

It's a little like getting on the Internet and floating like flotsam in the atmosphere. Information comes out of the air, bombarding you from every side. But without a focus, a targeted destination, you are still lost. Access to information will not save you.

Rerouting to the narrow road brings focus and salvation. There is no other road [John 14:6], and "no other name under heaven whereby we must be saved." [Acts 4:12] Even though much of my counseling has been done in so-called secular settings, I make my role as a *Christian* therapist clear. I know what works.

Even so, I draw the line at using any form of coercion or manipulation to influence the outcome. I respect and encourage my clients' power to choose for themselves by making it very clear what my role will and ought to be. *They* must determine their itinerary and destination points. That is what empowerment is all about. I would be doing my clients a great disservice by presuming to "rewrite their life script." It would also rob them of much of the joy of personal discovery.

Also, I have no wish to stand one day before the Great White Throne and take the heat for how someone else chooses to live their life. Each person must choose for him/herself. Each person must take responsibility. Then, and only then, will he/she find healing, wholeness and the power to choose and change his/her situation. Once the ground rules are set, we sit down together and examine troubling areas of their lives; we explore attitudes and aptitudes. I encourage them to clarify personal goals, so that, instead of life continuing to break down, they can choose God's path for their lives and begin anew, starting right where they are, with all their flaws and imperfections, here and now.

Chapter 2. "To Choose, or Not to Choose": What Kind of A Question Is That?

None of us wants to "suffer the slings and arrows of outrageous fortune," as Hamlet did. It just so happens that life's journey is full of inescapable and unpleasant road blocks, potholes, detours, roads that go nowhere and, worse, roads that lead to disaster and even death. It is a journey fraught with "dangers, toils and snares," as John Newton so aptly described it. But it is also possible to find God's amazing grace, even in the midst of our trials and griefs.

Tapping into God's saving strength doesn't just happen by accident; it happens by design. Because we *choose* to become a part of God's larger plan for our lives. That is why it's so important *how* you choose, *Who* you choose, and *what* you choose.

There is another question concerning choice that is often skirted, but must be addressed. This is the question of **non-choice.** Regardless of the pious trappings it may be decked out in, it is deeply rooted in unbelief and inevitably leads to destruction.

People frequently ask me, "*Why Must I Make Any Choice At All?*" Perhaps you've had it put to you as part of some friend's rationale for why life is the way it is. It usually comes as a two-part question: *What Real Choice Do I Have?* and *Won't the Outcome Be the Same, No Matter What I Do?* [Or, inferred, *Don't Do?*]

Sound familiar?..

These questions generally come from people whose lives resemble roadkill. You've met them. They have given up. Here's how their thinking goes: "*Hey, I'm not God. Since tragedy and hardship are no respecters of persons, why fight it? It's going to happen anyway (if it hasn't already), so why kid myself? It's out of my hands. The outcome is already decided. I can't do a thing to stop what's happening, or what is going to happen. I am merely a victim of fate, a walking time bomb, an accident waiting to happen.*

Ouch! Sounds like the Sixties all over again, with its kiss-life-goodbye-because-it's-too-late, flag burning, acid-dropping, hopeless philosophy of Leary and his followers. It's Nietzsche reheated and slopped on a sesame bun. It's unwholesome, defeating, and it's not new, folks. It's been around for a *long* time. (Read Proverbs and Ecclesiastes, before you dispute me on that!)

Yet these uncheery souls are not so very different from you and me. They at least know life is tough, that "stuff" happens, and that we aren't always in control. They are sufficiently in touch with reality to know what's going on.

But they are also not willing to invest anything of themselves in the outcome. They reason thus: If they *do* nothing [i.e., choose *not* to choose, or participate], nobody can blame them for what happens, right?

On the surface, this noncommittal approach may sound plausible. It certainly sounds safe, doesn't it?

I wouldn't count on it!

What really happens is that these hapless victims of their own thinking relinquish control. They let go of the reins and let that rough little pony called Life just stomp the daylights out of 'em. These dear people, male and female, come from every religious, ethnic, educational, and cultural background. There is a resignation here that is so tainted with cynicism and fatalism that they can actually sit there in my office and smile and shrug about their misfortune!

They put up with an abusive spouse, or dilapidated housing, or a job that forces them and their kids to walk around underfed and in rags. I am not exaggerating! And I am not talking about uneducated people either. Some of my clients have earned more degrees than I, but their lives are a mess. Those with jobs complain about work and co-workers, instead of examining what they could do to improve their own interpersonal communication skills.

Their physical appearance generally reflects an inner depression. Minor ailments continually plague them; they don't feel well, yet refuse to see a doctor for treatment. Something is always going wrong in these people's lives, not because they don't have ability, but because they are simply not willing to use their adult faith-faculty to think and evaluate what is ruling and impairing the choices they need to make. As a consequence, their experience of life is disappointing and substandard, deadly and dull to the extreme.

These are the fence-straddlers, the arm chair politicians, the "experts." They are critics and spectators, rather than players in the game of life. They are in the majority, I might add. They talk all the time about what's wrong, but they wind up doing nothing to extricate themselves and their loved ones from dire circumstances. Instead, they make all kinds of excuses for why things are the way they are.

It takes a bonfire of considerable heat to get these people up out of their chairs, and even then, they keep looking around for someone else to put out the fire!

Basically, they have a fatalistic slant on what we Christians call Predestination, which has to do with God choosing us, which He has from the very beginning. "For whom He did foreknow, He also did predestinate." [Romans 8:29] Only they leave out the key ingredient, faith.

God has already chosen us in Christ Jesus. [John 15:19; II Thessalonians 2:13] Now it's up to us. Will we choose God? Predestination does not make us puppets; far from it. Rather, the knowledge of God's unceasing, active concern for us is meant to free us to respond in kind.

It is impossible to be the recipient of God's active *agape* love and remain passive and indifferent. Just as a match set to kindling ignites a flame, His love *will* evoke an active and worthy response from those He has chosen.

Clearly, those who maintain a stance of passive resistance, avoiding choice and change, need to examine where they stand with the Lord. These are not necessarily "bad" people, in the sense that they are any worse than those who respond in faith. But they are, by an act of their will, blocking the flow of power needed to live well. The apostle James hit the nail squarely on the head when he wrote, "True faith is active." [*cf.* James 2:24] Any other kind is useless.

The uncommitted tend to believe their lack of commitment guarantees them the best of both worlds. They want it handed to them. They don't want to struggle (although wishing doesn't stop it from being part of the human experience). They don't want pain. They want material prosperity and peace and happiness, just like the rest of us. They just don't want to work for it! We generally associate this attitude with freeloaders and professional panhandlers. And we're not far wrong in thinking that.

Only problem is, a lot of people infected with the same virus are sitting in our church pews! And living down the street from us. They may even (ahem) be sitting in our favorite chair in front of the TV every night. They go to church just enough to get a "little religion," just enough to give them a bit of respectable spit and polish, but not enough to separate them from the world. They dabble their toes in the river of life, but never enough to place them in the full, rich stream of God's blessings.

James warned fence-straddlers: "A double-minded man is unstable in all his ways." [James 1:8]

You see, it *does* matter which side we are on. "No man can serve two masters," Jesus said. [Matthew 6:24; Luke 16:13]   The longer you live, the more obvious it should become that we all serve one master or another. Even if we live in a totalitarian system, we have a choice. Because what we are discussing here is a matter of the *will.*

Regardless of our circumstances, we can always choose how we respond, whether in love or hatred, whether in forgiveness or vengeful spite, whether in understanding or rejection. It is all a matter of what controls our spirit, or rather, I should say, *Who* is in control.

Every choice, every action we take spreads around us like a stone imploding upon the surface of a pond. With the world caught in a tidal wave of violence, hatred, divisions and mistrust, the imperative to choose, and choose wisely, takes on new urgency and new meaning.

We are in the heat of a spiritual battle. Our human condition has placed us at the forefront. We did not elect to be there, but we are. The flak and artillery, the bombs and bullets are flying all around us. We're cut off, hemmed in. Danger everywhere. No escape. We're wounded, we're hurting, we're vulnerable. We need back-up desperately, and soon, or we shall perish.

The radio receiver is in our hand. It's up to us to choose: Are we going to try to make it out on our bellies through the muck and misery of where life finds us? Or are we going to call for reinforcements? The choice is ours.

The decision we make is critical to the outcome. Most of us, regardless of how much we're hurting, are afraid to see the truth of our condition. None of us wants to view ourselves as sunk in the mire of combat. Pride tells us we ought to be able to make it in our strength. But we're fooling ourselves. We're no better than that lone dog soldier surrounded by land mines. Our need is no less great. We need God's strong arm and His grace to bring us safely home.

How successfully we complete our mission in life depends on how we respond to this one question: **Where do I choose to place my faith, as I travel this road?**

In myself and my meager resources?

Or in God?

Each choice we make creates a whole new set of choices or options, which in turn present more possibilities. Each step, each choice determines the path we follow and the success or failure of our quest.

Success is only found by facing our difficulties and pain head-on. That doesn't mean we should rush ahead into the dark, but *by faith,* we place one foot after the other, as God provides light for our path.

By our choices, we will either become stumbling blocks to our own progress and to others, or we can choose to be conduits through which the Light of the World may flow, lighting all the dark corners and bringing hope and healing to ourselves and our loved ones.

So the question is not, "How do we get out of making a choice," as some have supposed. The truth is, **we cannot *not* choose.** *Not to choose is to have already made a choice.*

When we forfeit our God-given right to choose, we pre-script ourselves for disaster. **We *must* choose.** For therein lies our only hope and salvation.

In the next few chapters, we shall examine mindsets and false assumptions we make about life, which hinder our progress along life's perilous journey. We will then contrast these with our freedom in Christ, so that we may *choose* and *act* in ways that bring benefit and blessing to us and to those around us.

Chapter 3. It's Our Choice: Tyranny or Freedom

Of course, choice goes both ways. You can choose to act, or not to act. Your decisions and actions are generally based upon belief systems harbored deep within your soul. Sometimes these don't coincide with the beliefs you verbally espouse. You may honestly adhere to all the correct Christian tenets and doctrines. You may give evidence to this by regular church attendance, tithing, teaching Sunday school, serving on various boards and committees, and any number of worthwhile philanthropic activities. These are all commendable, and when the inner life is consistent with the outward representation, harmony and fruitful manifestations of the presence of God show up within all facets of an individual's life.

Unfortunately—and the torn fabric of American life attests to this fact—all is not well with the vast majority of our population today. Statistics indicate a rampant disregard for human life, increased family discord; higher rates of illegitimacy; illiteracy, and single parent households; lowered educational and moral standards; soaring crime rates, including rape, gang involvement, drug trafficking, drive-by shootings, the "recreational" use of cocaine, and white collar crime, just to mention a few.

These tragic statistics call into serious question the true inner condition of many who call themselves Christians. The lackluster complacency and dullness of their lives is neither attractive nor energized by any genuine power from the Source of all light and life. For this reason, it's important to examine what I call **The Tyrannies of Not Choosing**, and then contrast each tyranny with **The Freedoms Nurtured by Choosing Life.**

A. The Tyranny of Belonging or Fitting In, vs. The Freedom of Choosing Not to Fit In.

Contrary to what most people think, playing it safe and trying to conform to externally imposed standards are no more conducive to good mental or spiritual health than anarchy is to improving public safety. One has only to observe crowd behavior to see how lost the individual becomes as he/she becomes swept up in the heat of the moment. The horrific results of shared mob mentality demean and devalue each individual part of the whole.

This is, of course, an extreme example of what can occur when individuals surrender what is an essential and an integral part of themselves in order to fit in with others. But be that group comprised of family members, a corporate structure, labor union, church body, club or collective community, in each case there are certain well defined rules and expectations. There are also punishments and consequences for those who step over the line by looking, behaving or—heaven forbid! —daring to express an opposing view.

However subtle the forms of manipulation and management may be, these group systems impose external controls that send a message that poses the threat of extinction to that inner light that represents the truest essence of our human spirit, the part of us that pipes up as a kid and tells the world, "Hey, that's me!"

Over a period of time, this little "kid" often takes a terrible beating. He/she either conforms or gets pounded into shape. This is most often done by Do-Gooders, who assert that they are only acting in the best interests of the child. (Example: The pressures brought to bear by high priests and priestesses of political correctness.) In actual fact, these Do-Gooders are more interested in eliminating nuisances and anything startling or different. The message is really: *Don't make waves.*

When we become a party to this unamusing game of conformity, either as a victim or a perpetrator, nobody wins. In fact, a lot of the joy and zest for living is missed.

One of the great joys of my family in recent years was getting to know a young man named David. He was as genuine a Christian as you could hope to meet.

Over six feet eight and a true giant, David was never timid or apologetic about his size. Very early, he had learned what it meant to stand out and be "different;" there was nothing he could do about it, although it had to have been painful for a young boy taunted by classmates. As his professional resume later declared to the world, life had taught him to be "infinitely patient." He summed himself up thus: "Suffers fools gladly."

Despite rejection and misunderstandings often engendered by his size, unusually bright wit, and keen intellect, David refused to allow himself to be squeezed into the mold or flattened by adversity. He was a strong, compelling presence wherever he went, simply because he knew who he was and refused to be less.

He knew how to make an entrance—oh, boy, did he! At first meeting, some people thought he was eccentric, but that didn't squelch his delightful love of life or his good humor. He couldn't haul his huge frame around inconspicuously, so he didn't try. He drove a customized motorcycle, built to accommodate his hugeness, and being an imaginative young man of ready wit—a brilliant mind, actually—he often wore a cape and boots to complement his black helmet.

Seeing him rumble down the street, friends lovingly dubbed him, "Captain Marvel." He was outlandishly theatrical on occasion, but never took himself too seriously. He loved life passionately, but lived a life that was a credit to his parents and, I might add, to his Lord.

28

David was generous with his time, tutoring kids in math and computer science. He led Bible studies, composed Christian music, sang with a band, and loved to challenge anything phony. He also had a degree in Bible and was working on his Master's Degree at Multnomah Bible College and was actively involved in ministry.

He was a total original, startling and controversial, a brilliant comet that streaked across the Las Vegas desert skyline. He made the Strip lighting dim by comparison.

You notice that I use the past tense. At age thirty-one, David lay down in the middle of the day for a nap and passed into the presence of His Lord for eternity. He wasn't ill; he was just ready. He had learned the secret of life, sucked the juice out of life here on earth. What we were privileged to experience in David was a totally unique individual, who chose to live life to the fullest each day. He was the perfect antidote for predictable, dull conformity.

What I came to see and admire in David was his irrepressible joy. Nobody could take it away from him.

Selfishly, my only complaint is that David was in such a hurry. He didn't waste a minute. He had a date to keep with God. He was—and *is*, for I look forward to meeting him again—one of those incredibly spontaneous Christians who holds nothing back. His boldness in Christ left the rest of us with our mouths open.

While we're on the subject of his death, I might as well be completely up front. There are times when there are no answers. Probably none of us will never know why David died. Or why so many of his dreams for the future went unfulfilled. But I can say this much with certainty: When we get to heaven, we're going to be so glad to see him, it won't matter why.

"*Why?*" is probably the one question that sidetracks and confuses the issue more frequently than any other. We don't need to know why. We just need to know that God loves David and the situation's under control.

Now, returning to the subject of conformity, I am not for one minute suggesting that we all don a cape, rush right out and buy an enormous three-wheel chrome motorcycle and tear down the highway like David.

If you must seek conformity, be conformed to Christ. [Romans 8:29]   Attempts to copy one's peers produce an imitation, the last thing a "character" like David would encourage. What I *do* urge is for you to take time to discover your own uniqueness and develop it.   Dare to be yourself, instead of yielding to the pressures of conformity which stultify and deaden. Instead of attempting to march to someone else's drumbeat—always a big mistake—find your own inner rhythms and tempo.

Try to view yourself with the same sense of pleasure God must have experienced when he engineered the events surrounding your birth. He created you special.

You *are* special.   Don't let anyone or anything rob you of the joy and the freedom that comes with being you.

"Be not conformed to this world: but be transformed by the renewing of your mind, that you may prove what is that good and acceptable and perfect will of God." [Romans 12:2]

B. The Tyranny of Trying to Figure Out Craziness vs. Knowing the Truth about Ourselves.

All of us have experienced the tyranny of craziness or crazymaking. It may have been trying to figure out what an adult authority figure, possibly a parent, teacher or sometimes even a spouse, actually wanted from us. For the purpose of discussion, let's use this possible example of a teacher-pupil engaged in crazymaking:

As the pupil, we have put forth our best effort, thinking that we know exactly what we are supposed to do to get an A on a spelling assignment our third grade teacher gave us. We confidently hand in the home-work and—*kaboom!* To our complete and utter dismay, we learn the teacher expected us to disregard the printed instructions at the top of the paper and write a descriptive sentence using each of the spelling words listed. She took off an extra two points for every object we colored in our eagerness to please. Like most kids, we sit there stunned. We tried so hard, but we just couldn't win.

Even though we now knew how to spell each word on the piece of paper correctly, we had gone about it all wrong; therefore, the entire exercise is incorrect. We are a failure. The teacher has played "Gotcha!" and our buying into her crazy little game has earned us a "D" or an "F."

There are so many variations of this game, including nit-picking, that it would be impossible to go into them all. There are books devoted to the subject, in case you haven't had your fill of crazymaking or need further clarification. What you need to realize here is that a great many people specialize in making people around them crazy. They go through life playing games of "Gotcha!" and One-Up-Manship. Getting suckered into this is particularly deadly if you buy into the underlying sickness this breeds.

A couple of years ago, a young woman come to me, confessing suicidal tendencies. Eydie was an attractive adver-tising executive in her late twenties. She had been married only a few months to Ben, a handsome professional man who had taken particular pains to sweep her off her feet. They both came from Christian homes, but like a great many active singles, had allowed themselves to become sidetracked by exciting careers and the social scene.

When they met, Eydie and Ben both expressed an interest in having a family and re-establishing ties with the church in order to create the right climate for raising children. However, when I saw the wife about six months into the marriage, she no longer entertained any thoughts of having a family. Her relationship with Ben had become so strained that her every thought was centered on escape.

"If I can't get away from him, I'll go crazy," she told me during the initial tearful interview. "I've tried leaving him, but he always talks me into coming back. If things go on this way much longer, I'm afraid of what I may do." She blurted out that Ben had systematically weaned her from her circle of friends and created a breach in her relationship with her family.

Her first marriage at twenty had ended in divorce. Her fear of criticism, should this second marriage fail, set her up emotionally for the power games that ensued. Besides going behind her back to her friends and planting false impressions of his own insecurity and suspicions that Eydie might be seeing other men behind his back, Ben had begun to drink heavily.

During these weekend binges, he began to abuse her physically and emotionally. He confined her physically to the house or bedroom on a number of occasions. Once or twice, she climbed out a window and tried to escape on foot, only to have him pursue her and drag her back.

Ben was careful not to drink during the work week when it could effect his position. But on weekends, he systematically went through her belongings, threw out Eydie's photo albums and other memorabilia, thereby destroying her connections with the past and with meaningful relationships that affirmed her as a worthwhile and valued person.

Under my questioning, Eydie admitted that her family had never been anything but supportive of her, despite her disastrous first marriage. She also kept trying to make sense out of her present husband's behaviors and irrational jealousies.

She had also fallen into the mistake of blaming her friends for believing Ben's accusations of infidelity. In a relatively short time, her thinking had become so muddled that she actually felt betrayed by her girl friends, instead of trusting herself to sort through the data, see the truth, and act in her own best interests. As a result of her expressed anger toward her friends, many had washed their hands of her. This had only made her easier prey during what followed.

After a particularly violent row, she showed up on her parents' doorstep at four in the morning. She was, by her own admission, a wreck. She had lost twenty pounds, her skin was sallow, her eyes a wild haunted blue. A few hours later, Ben phoned and "reasoned" with her, making her feel that if only she didn't upset him so much, he wouldn't be driven to drink to excess. "What we need is a baby, so you'll feel fulfilled and stay home," he told her.

Because Eydie genuinely wanted her marriage to succeed, she got back into her car and went back to him. Two days later, she phoned her parents in a panic, enlisting their help to move her personal effects out of the house. This they did, welcoming her into the sanctuary of their home.

But in hours, again Eydie was accepting a dinner date with her estranged husband, who proceeded to show her the error of her ways, that her family was actually responsible for breaking them up.

Seeing his point, Eydie unleashed an angry tirade on her family for their so-called "interference" and lack of sympathy, whereupon she reconciled with Ben again. By this time, she was about five months into the marriage. Her body was starting to feel the strain of sleeplessness, followed by narco-leptic symptoms. She nearly drove off the road on the way to work one morning, and almost wished she had. However, the thought that she might unconsciously be fulfilling some hidden agenda of her husband's wrenched her back from the path of destruction. Thoughts of suicide spurred even more self-condemnation and guilt.

"I'm really trying to make this marriage work," she told me earnestly, wringing a tissue in her hands, which were never still. My question was, what was Ben doing to the woman he had promised to love, cherish and protect, "till death do us part"? Sitting in my office was a young woman who felt that even coming to a counselor was an act of betrayal, when in actual fact, she had been worked over emotionally and physically, as systematically as any sparring partner in the boxing ring.

Even in her confused state, Eydie was still able to choose life over death. Deep down, she wanted to know the truth: Was she the terrible person her husband made her out to be, or was she still a child of God? Was there any hope for her marriage? Would her family and friends—and that included her Best Friend, Jesus—ever be able to forgive her? She had said some hurtful things in the heat of anxiety and fear of failure.

With her decision to disassociate herself from the lies and distortions and manipulations that had reduced her to emotional ruin, Eydie quickly reconnected with the Source of power, her Lord. She sought forgiveness for real, not imagined, sins committed against her family and friends. She divorced her husband after realizing that Ben was repeating abusive patterns modeled by his alcoholic father and saintly mother, who endured lifelong abuse in the name of wifely submission. (Far from providing a healthy Christian example for her children, this dear mother's resignation had actually facilitated her husband's sickness.)

There was one other rather fascinating aspect to this case: Eydie's company life insurance policy listed Ben as sole beneficiary in the event of her death. While I prefer not to read too much into any ulterior motives, I am grateful that Eydie chose freedom, rather than continue to subject herself to the tyranny of crazymaking.

"You shall know the truth, and the truth shall set you free." [John 8:32]

Chapter 4. Magical Thinking

C. The Tyranny of Erroneous Expectation vs. The Freedom of Acceptance

I have already mentioned the problem therapists have with clients who persist in "magical thinking" with regard to their own treatment. Unfortunately, this tendency to look to others for solutions which must primarily be found within oneself is not all that rare. It is instilled in us from the moment we open our little mouth in hunger and realize how dependent upon others we are for our very survival.

We submit to the inconveniences and tyrannies of parents and caretakers in order to survive. We conform to and accommodate the expectations of others (teachers, babysitters, doctors, etc.) out of the very selfish yet valid desire to get our needs met. We also begin to believe a great many "myths" that are passed down to us, often in nonverbal messages, about ourselves and about those we seek to fit in with. [You will note in our discussion that one tyranny frequently overlaps into other sick manifestations, which hinder our progress ultimately.]

Our ability to sort out information becomes tainted very early. We are told we must do this or that, in order to fit in with others, and that is all well and good. However, most attempts to indoctrinate us into belief systems are imposed upon us, rather than our own by choice.

We accept lies along with truth, and before very long, we swallow a great many lies. We become victims of "wishful thinking," because "if only" is easier than recognizing the pain we are in and the pain in the neck we may be to others. We want to believe we are loved by our fellow travelers, even if we are not. We seek ways to earn love, to feel important and worthwhile. If we cannot find acceptance and love "as is," our "critical parent" tells us we must measure up.

That critical parent is at first external but soon becomes internalized, as we accept the opinion of others about ourselves. If we resemble our father, who has run off with another woman, we may experience rejection from our mother, who in her hurting condition transfers her anger and disapproval to the child.

We are puzzled but sufficiently aware to recognize that something is wrong with us. We then begin to compensate and perform in ways that (we hope) will earn our mother's favor. Of course, we are doomed, because no matter how well we behave, we still look like "dear old Dad," the bane of her existence. The magical thinking comes about through an unrealistic expectation, that we will somehow find love from others by performing.

This erroneous expectation escalates as we grow older. More sophisticated rules come into play, as we try to fit into social groups. Our peers at school, and later at college, impose new sets of rules and expectations, which we must either fall in with, or else we will fall out of their favor.

Deep down inside, there is this sense of longing, this hidden shame, that somehow we ought to be able to measure up. We want love so desperately, but we're never quite good enough. We work harder; we do a terrific job; we're passed over on the next promotion. Always disappointed, because the reason for our striving is rooted in our insecurity and a sense of unworthiness. We double our efforts; we buy *more* lies, about ourselves and the world around us. We want so desperately for life to be different, but it isn't.

Our efforts to compensate, to shut out the pain, continue. Some drink too much, in order not to feel their sense of isolation, even in a crowd. They sleep with people they don't even care about. Or they gamble, because it gives them a temporary sense of power and control, and because people (laboring under erroneous expectations of their own) will notice and admire them for the few seconds it takes to bet everything at the craps table or throw down a couple of wild cards at poker and rake in the pot. They are looking for some way to win. Some way to feel appreciated and loved.

But the guilt and the emptiness inside continue to grow. We are lost. We keep striving for that sense of worth, or identification as a person worth loving. Only we don't know what it is we're searching for. We only know the laughter's hollow, and life isn't getting any better.

Always performing. Never really getting the message, that it isn't really important what others think.

This is the tragedy of erroneous expectations We haven't faced the truth about the damage sin does to relationships and to the human spirit. We are always reacting, never acting. Which isn't so surprising. Our view of life has become as distorted as everyone's around us.

Everyone is waiting to win the lottery, or find the perfect mate who will make everything wonderful and perfect for us. We are just sure if we can only figure out the boss, we will get that bonus. If we buy the right car or acquire enough of the right adult "toys," people will admire and look up to us. We will be a success, if we only do thus and so. *Then* we will be happy. *Then* we will be loved.

Only it doesn't work that way. And slowly disillusion-ment replaces false optimism. We become cynical. We fill our lives with materialism. We lose ourself in recreational vices. Or we throw ourselves into more busyness at the office, or at church. Still striving for acceptance. Still trying to earn recognition and love.

We end up living an endless, unrewarding lie. All for the benefit of others, who are probably too wrapped up in their own distorted thinking to realize how badly *we* hurt.

In all of this, the child in us continues to struggle against the smothering effects of all this activity and inner toil. He wants to breathe, to survive. And this leads to self-absorption, so that even admirable deeds—for not all people plagued by erroneous expectations are drawn to vice—become contaminated by ulterior motives.

The apostle Paul knew something of this when he warned Christians, "Though I give my body to be burned, if I have not love, it profits me nothing." [I Corinthians 13:3] We must remember that in his unconverted state, Paul was a Pharisee among Pharisees, a man of extraordinary zeal and pride. There is little doubt in my mind that Paul knew firsthand the futility of performing for the approval of others.

Here was a man who stood by during the stoning of Stephen. You can't tell me he didn't ask himself, somewhere during his persecution of the early followers of Jesus, just how far his lust for power and recognition , both symptomatic of a driving need for love, would take him.

I do not minimize the action of the Holy Spirit in breaking Paul down and bringing him to his senses, but it is not hard to see how many manifestations of the tyranny of erroneous expectation are present in the world. It infects blatant sinners and staid churchgoers alike.

What these people all have in common is the Great Cover-up. They can't tell it like it is, because they can't face the truth, that life is simply not the way they were brought up to believe.

Victims of this thinking frequently transfer their frustration and anger into devaluing others, often self-righteously claiming to know what is best for others. They demand perfection of others, out of a need to justify themselves against a deep, even unconscious sense of failure.

They strive, yet Utopia—in this case, a sense of completion and love—continues to elude them. Strive as they must, they always have a sense of frustration and failure, because the expectation is never quite realized.

Untreated, these people may become overwhelmed with hopelessness and depression; prostrate with exhaustion and the futility of a lifetime spent trying to earn and grasp that ever elusive "thing" [love and acceptance]. They may even throw in the towel. Bitterness and great anger boil just below the surface in these people, although they are often unable to acknowledge this. Instead, the first symptoms I observe on an initial visit may be immobility, an almost paralysis of the spirit.

We can glean much wisdom from the Parable of the Prodigal Son. The self-righteous brother's perception of his brother's lost condition was correct. Like the rest of the family, he must have felt keenly the pain and disgrace visited upon the entire family by his brother's moral failure and selfishness.

His mistake was in not seeing how needy he himself was. Somewhere along the way, he had made a conscious choice to cut himself off from his prodigal brother. Whether his brother's actions were too painful, personally humiliating, or downright expensive, he soon lost sight of what God finds lovable in every prodigal—boldness, curiosity, a sense of adventure.

Actually, both brothers had erroneous expectations.

The Prodigal Son had erroneous expectations about *everything:* His view of how the world would receive him, as he squandered his fortune, led to disillusionment and self-hatred. When he finally "came to himself," he still had no idea how his Father would receive him. His perceptions of his true condition so overwhelmed him that he failed to grasp the fact that **his Father loved him, as is!**

Meanwhile, back at the ranch, the well behaved Righteous Brother was as much a prodigal beneath his proper exterior as his errant scallywag of a brother, wallowing in the pigsties of life. For one thing, he had the erroneous expectation that he could *earn* the Father's love through righteous deeds and circumspect living. In actual fact, there was nothing wrong with his outward performance as a dutiful son. I am sure his Father was pleased with his loyalty.

But festering beneath this veneer of propriety was a troubled young man, unable to love generously, because somehow he had allowed his incorrect assumptions about his Father's love to spill over into his attitude toward his younger brother. The Righteous Prodigal was not enjoying the full fellowship available to him from the Father, and one can only wonder what, in his interactions with his brother, may have caused the younger brother to seek his inheritance and move out!

How many of us are like these two!

Whichever brother we may more closely relate to should not be our central concern here, however. Both suffered from distorted thinking.

What *is* important for us to see is that **God loves us, as is!** We have His Word on that. If you grasp nothing else from this parable, hammer this into your head: *"By grace [God's unmerited favor] are you saved, and not by your own efforts; it is the gift of God, not of works, lest any should boast."* [Ephesians 2:8, 9] Once this truth sinks in, life will never be the same. You will be able to discard the Biggest Lie of all, that you somehow must measure up to some impossible standard in order to be loved. Get that out of your head right now. **You *are* loved, just as you are.**

A word of caution: We may at vulnerable times feel drawn back into former erroneous expectations and assumptions. Do not despair! Our God is a loving God, and He is also an *attentive* God, guarding each of us as carefully as any good Shepherd from the storms and perils of living.

When we find ourselves slipping about on the narrow ledge of "magical thinking," or tumbling from the craggy heights through our inattention, or the misplacing of our trust, or becoming involved with the wrong people, of *course*, there are consequences. But from the instant we recognize and confess our need, from the instant we cry out to God, we are no longer alone in the battle. He is there to do for us what we in ourselves are powerless to accomplish.

Remember! All power belongs to the Lord. [Psalm 62:11; Matthew 28:18] Any man-made success or accomplishment is only a cheap counterfeit of God's power.

"His hand is not shortened, that it cannot save." [Isaiah 59:1] What a sublime way of expressing the *active* nature of God's love toward us! He doesn't merely cluck his tongue and shake his head sympathetically when we, His children, are hurt and struggling. *Regardless* of the reason we are in the condition we are in, He is active in His compassion.

Even when our dilemma is the direct result of our own wilful behavior, or even our stupidity, God still gives us a choice: We can either trust and call upon Him, or we may continue to walk in our own strength—and take the consequences.

Because I believe we all need to beware of taking the grace of God for granted, I must relate the following story:

In my counseling ministry, I am sometimes called upon to do extended therapy with entertainers on the Las Vegas Strip. Most of these people are ordinary people, not nearly as glamorous as the tabloids suggest. They work hard for their living, only instead of lifting a shovel, or selling office supplies, they just happen to rehearse like fanatics to perfect themselves as musicians, athletes, comics; they work terrible hours, and so forth.

One such client was a trapeze artist, Sol. He was a very attractive, powerfully built man, known in the United States and Europe to be one of the best in the business. He had a beautiful wife. He had a nice house and car. He had job security, a long contract with one of the shows in town. Seemingly, he had everything to live for.

Yet from the minute Sol set foot inside my office, he spoke of nothing but his plans to commit suicide. Stored up inside this man was an inordinate amount of anger, which he was perfectly willing to examine and talk about. He hadn't had a pleasant childhood, but it was certainly no worse than many.

The many emblems of his international success gave testimony to his high and exacting expectations of himself. He was a hyper-critical perfectionist and difficult to live with. He was a man driven by the need to achieve, and still it wasn't enough. He had all the classic signs of burned-out "magical thinking;" he had come to the end of his rope, he told me. Because his threats were taken seriously, his therapy included a period of hospitalization, medical treatment for clinical depression, and intensive personal counseling.

But there was within this man such a deep-seated self-hatred that he couldn't accept the idea that God could love what he did not—that is, himself. To many, this man's feelings of rejection might seem like merely a projection of the negative authority father figure of his past. But it went deeper than that. This man did not merely agree with his father's exacting assessment of him; he presumed to place himself in the role of a judging God, a very dangerous and arrogant decision on his part. We met a number of times, but he couldn't be dissuaded from this unhealthy obsession with death, even though he saw how it was tearing his wife and children apart emotionally.

A few years elapsed following our last session, when his wife unexpectedly telephoned to let me know he had committed suicide in the hotel parking garage where she worked.

The wife was in a shock of remorse. Why hadn't she been able to talk him out of it? Where had she failed? Had her love meant nothing to him? His suicidal talk was nothing new, of course; he had threatened suicide for years. She was nearly overcome with grief, as, indeed, Sol had carefully planned, even making sure she would find his body when she left work at the end of her shift. Essentially, he chose to be his own Judge and Executioner. His Final Act revealed a high degree of malevolent, possibly even demonic activity. Thus, he destroyed a successful career and did irreparable harm to his wife and children.

Sadly, Sol found it easier to carry out his own destruction than to admit his fallibility, his desperate need for God or anyone else. [To a lesser degree, this is not uncommon among those whose pride stands in the way of repentance.]

Suicide is never a viable option. God would have forgiven Sol and cleansed him of his dark, obsessive thoughts, if he had been willing to admit his need. But alas for human pride! Sol, like the son of perdition, chose not to be saved. This, then, demonstrates the ultimate pay-off of those who persist in fostering erroneous expectations.

Fortunately, not all attempts at suicide succeed. Ropes do break, and bullets misfire. I have treated two young men who shot themselves in the head and lived to face the stunning fact that God had other plans for them.

One man, feeling trapped and desperate because of a cocaine habit, shot himself in the side of the head. The bullet exited the other side of his skull, leaving him with an occasional headache to remind him of his folly. "I was a fool to think God couldn't help me deal with my drug problem," he told me. "Today, I am drug free and back on track. I'm getting married in June, and I have a good job with a public utility company."

The other young man shot himself in the frontal lobe. The bullet lodged in his sinuses, and he wound up having corrective surgery for a deviated septum. After intensive physical therapy and counseling, as part of his sentencing he now shares his testimony with local school kids about the dangers of mind-altering drugs.

Neither of these young men would encourage others to try avoiding pain by taking such drastic measures. Most people who try suicide, if they are serious about it, generally succeed. If someone you know is contemplating suicide, take *immediate* steps to intervene.

Some dysfunctional families create a different type of suicidal pattern. Many years ago, when I was pastoring a church in Illinois, a woman approached me for counseling. Mrs. Emmett, a college-educated woman, was married to a professional man. Several members of his family were active in politics; they had money and were well connected socially.

Childless for many years, the Emmetts had finally adopted a son, Sid, who was active in scouting and eventually became an Eagle Scout. As I became involved in the family's dynamics, the emotional climate of the marriage soon became apparent. Both parents were engaged in an unhealthy co-dependency that was psychologically and emotionally harmful. The husband was overly controlling, the wife continually struggling for emotional survival, while the son, as time went on, gravitated toward escape through drugs.

After several months of ill health, the husband died in his mid-fifties. Within weeks, an insidious pattern emerged. Instead of accepting her new-found freedom as a blessing, Mrs. Emmett allowed twenty years of guilt and repressed anger to build up inside, until her desire to go on living was over-powered by remorse. [This is akin to the guilt often felt by survival victims.] Within a few weeks, Mrs. Emmett was spending most of her time in bed. Soon she was hospitalized with a mysterious gastric ailment. Nothing clinically wrong, yet her physical condition continued to deteriorate. After about two months, she, too, died.

An autopsy revealed nothing that could account for her death. It was one of the oddest cases I have ever encountered in my practice. The woman simply chose not to go on, but to join her husband in death!

Sadly enough, in the months following her demise, her son

became heavily involved in drugs; he died of an overdose within the year. Here was a family, whose erroneous expectations had so crippled each other, that the situation eventually played itself out in a triple "suicide."

If there is a lesson to be learned from this bizarre and tragic story, it is to beware of the pervasiveness of sin within any social system. Jesus likened it to the spread of a little leaven (a symbol for sin) until it infects the whole.

These case histories should warn us about the seriousness of persisting in erroneous expectations and "magical thinking." However, I am happy to report that not all victims of this type thinking remain "stuck." Now let's examine what happens when the power of addiction is broken.

Breaking the Power of Addiction

Ministering in Las Vegas, I encounter many people who are locked into compulsive behaviors. Gamblers are among this curious breed, always believing in magic, refusing to examine the evidence, trying to play "hot shot" for the recognition and love they hope it will gain them.

Of course, if we use our adult faith-faculty, we realize that slot machines are rigged. There isn't a card or a dice game at the casinos that hasn't been analyzed and modified to favor the house. Yet gamblers will bet their entire paycheck, sell groceries and the kid's formula and household furnishings, even their bodies, for a stake in the next game.

But occasionally God gets hold of one of these strange nightbirds, and when He does, it's exciting to watch the transformation.

When Fran first came to Las Vegas, she was divorced, broke, a long way from her home in New York, and desperate for work. After working as a shill, she landed a job as a dealer of 21. With her earnings, she was able to buy a modest house.

But then she became infected with the gambling "virus." [Notice the quotation marks; I in no way believe we can avoid responsibility for our actions, however addictive and compulsive.] Now, as an "insider" working at the casino tables every night, Fran had the "straight scoop" about gambling. She knew it was possible to come up with an occasional winning combination in 21: Just never go over 21. She started playing now and then after work.

Gradually her desire to win and her belief in her ability to win took over. She would stay in the casino from the end of her shift and play straight through until her next shift began. She began to lose large sums of money. She went through her savings. She began to borrow. She played with other customers' money and lost. She played for markers, racking up thousands of dollars of debt.

Then the collection goons came knocking at her door. She hid out. A messed-up face she didn't want. A one-way trip down a desert wash she didn't want. She couldn't show her face around the casinos, so she lost her job. She became afraid to leave her house, for fear someone might be following her. She was even afraid she might bump into the bookie she owed money to at the grocery store around the corner.

She lost weight. She threw up just thinking about what was going to happen when her creditors caught up with her.

Fran was not a Christian. She had gone a time or two to Sunday school as a child, but that was about all the exposure to the Gospel she had ever had.

She was up the proverbial creek, headed through the rapids without a paddle. Close enough to the falls to hear the crash of water against rock. No use kidding herself: She was going to die, if she didn't get herself turned around in time.

Only problem was, Fran didn't have the will or the strength to say no to her habit. Things had gotten so bad that she couldn't pass by the laundromat without betting customers which machine would spin-dry first. She was hooked. Her house was in foreclosure. She had hocked her car. She had bought the gun she planned to use to end her life.

The gun was in her hand, halfway to her temple, when she broke down and wept. "I can't even kill myself. Help me, God! I can't go on like this anymore."

It was the prayer of a powerless person. One who had lost the will to go on. By her own admission, she didn't deserve a second chance. She was middle-aged; she was plain and dumpy. Nobody paid attention to her, except when she had money to spend.

Nobody cared—except God.

And that day He sent her a caller. A Christian woman on her way home from a prayer meeting stalled her car outside Fran's house.

Fran still doesn't know what made her get up off her knees in her living room and walk to the front door. "The place was a mess. *I* was a mess. The last thing in the world I wanted was to open that door."

But she did. The woman explained her predicament and asked if she could telephone her husband. Standing in the doorway, Fran had to admit the phone company had cut off her service. Instead of going next door, the woman struck up a conversation, and the next thing Fran knew, she was being invited to a church potluck dinner!

Fran was fairly sure the woman had spotted her gun. She was waiting for her to "freak" and hightail it back to the safety of her car. But her caller just kept talking about Jesus and what a difference He had made in her life—and did Fran know Jesus?

Fran admitted that she didn't, adding that it wasn't likely He'd want anything to do with someone like her. She began to pile on the excuses, trying to drive the woman off, because she wouldn't be able to commit suicide if she went to the potluck, and she knew she'd lose her nerve if she postponed committing suicide much longer.

The woman simply wouldn't stop talking about Jesus! Finally Fran let herself get talked into going to the potluck. She introduced the woman, whose name was Betty, to her neighbor, Tina, who let Betty use the phone. While they waited for the husband to arrive, the three women continued to converse. In no time, Fran realized that both women were Christians.

She was floored by their interest and concern. Their acceptance and non-judgmental attitude broke through her fears. Her future still looked bleak, but with their encouragement, she prayed a simple sinner's prayer and was gloriously saved, that same afternoon!

Fran's problems and her addiction to gambling and other compulsive habits like smoking and drinking didn't vanish overnight. But she had taken the first step: She chose Jesus.

Three years later, she had paid off the debts with the help of a credit counselor. She was forty-three, living in a rented room, and having the time of her life. For the first time in her life she felt truly free! She was involved in several ministries of the church, including home Bible study. And when God laid it on her heart to do volunteer mission work in another city, she did so with the financial backing and loving prayers of her church family.

That gun may have had a bullet with Fran's name on it five years before, but God had other plans. "When God comes knocking at the door of your heart, it only makes sense to open up," Fran tells anyone who will listen. "His love will never let you down."

I don't think anything more needs to be said about the Power of Acceptance operating in a needy sinner's heart.

God's acceptance and love can be ours. We can't earn it; we don't deserve it. All we have to do is reach out and receive it in the Person of His Son Jesus.

Chapter 5. A Major Impediment in Our Path

D. The Tyranny of Worry, vs.
The Freedom to Decide and Act on Truth

It's important to recognize that attempts to avoid are frequently rooted in unfounded fears. Most of our fears prove to be mere hot air, but they do sidetrack and immobilize people from the business of living.

Worry is an compulsive obsession and totally nonproductive. People don't like to hear this, but worry comes from a refusal to trust God; it reflects our unwillingness to rely on the empowerment of God.

Jesus tells us, "The Father knows what you need, even before you ask Him." [Matthew 6:8] When we stew and work ourselves into a lather over what hasn't even happened, we are basically calling God a liar.

Worry distracts us from trusting God for our needs. It paralyzes and limits our participation in life and our choices. Distractions of this kind keep us unfocused, so that our attention and energies flit continually from one "what if" to another, never resolving anything. The sooner we confront this habit, which is based in unreality, the quicker we can free ourselves from the crippling paralysis of indecision.

Obsessiveness and compulsion narrow and restrict our focus, exerting and imposing bondage on the human spirit. It is astounding how much of our energy is wasted on unfounded fears and dangers that do not exist. It's like riveting our eyes and attention to a dot on the wall. We wind up not seeing anything else that's going on around us. It imposes a kind of tunnel vision, so that we cannot see reality and act upon it. Worry and obsessions and fears shut us down, so that our thinking, our ability to evaluate, make decisions and take action is impaired. It gravitates toward an increasingly narrow mindset that limits and overlooks the possibilities, especially in relation to letting the power of God work freely in our situation.

There are many forms of obsessive, compulsive and addictive behavior. Obsessions perceive all of life as a threat. Most obsessions involve a degree of paranoia and can be traced to the desire to avoid pain and responsibility.

A very gifted man, Max drove away all his friends with his obsessive, compulsive paranoia. Any time he visited friends and family members, he insisted that their house be thoroughly checked for "bugs." He just *knew* that everywhere he went, "they" had planted "bugs" and that "they" were following him, listening in on phone calls, and interfering with his ability to find and keep a job. Over a period of several years, he developed a full blown delusional system, based upon the belief that a worldwide conspiracy existed. "They" were pursuing him and investing an enormous amount of time, personnel and money to spy on him.

The elaborate scenario Max had created for himself reveals an overactive imagination, but more than that, a brilliant mind. He was very convincing. Friends were intimidated into playing along with his charades out of fear that he might be driven over the brink. People hooked on delusional obsessions are often quite brilliant.

Ironically, Max went through a prodigal experience and felt strongly convicted by the Holy Spirit many years ago. Nevertheless, he chose to reject Christ's claims on his life.

Obsessive people are caught in a survival mode, where life becomes a continual series of cliff hangers. When I was in clinical training years ago, I counseled a man who professed to be a Christian. Like Max, Kim also had a paranoid delusion that people were watching his every move wherever he went. Because he planned a trip to Las Vegas with his wife, I gave him an assignment, which he agreed to carry out. Kim was to carry a notebook and write down *in detail* every incident of people watching him in the casinos. He was to record descriptions, locations, times, circumstances, and his own behavior.

The results of this assignment jarred Kim into reality. He returned with an empty notebook, after realizing that no one had paid any attention to him, except his wife and those who provided him with service at the hotel. Recognizing this freed him , and he soon found his faith empowered to make healthy choices.

Choosing not to worry or be controlled by obsessive compulsions or delusional thinking frees us to live victoriously. Those who choose not to avoid, but to face affliction and difficulty, experience the power to live through life's pain. Discovering this new freedom reshapes their lives, so that they can become a new creation in Christ.

"Old things pass away; all things become new." [II Corinthians 5:17] As Christ imparts this new life to us, we find ourselves emerging victoriously from experiences that would otherwise reduce us to dust.

Numerous examples can be cited of people who have come through the fires of suffering and pain through placing their trust in God instead of their fears.

One such person is Andy, a young man born with disabilities that have kept him confined to a wheelchair and made him dependent upon others to feed and dress him from birth. Despite many trials and tribulations, he has developed a powerful faith that sees him through, day by day. Andy admits to experiencing fears, anxiety, and frustration, because of his many limiting infirmities. He has also known periods of great loneliness and isolation. Family members shunted him off to a nursing facility at an early age. He rarely has contact with his family, even on his birthday, Christmas and other holidays. And because of the setting in which he lives, he rarely has a chance to meet and converse with other young people.

Even so, Andy manages not to give in to self-pity and despair. Instead, he cultivates friendships with other patients at the nursing facility. He attends a nearby church faithfully, where he participates in worship, singing God's praises from his wheelchair and inviting other patients to attend. One of his great joys is being asked to take the offering or lead in prayer. As often as he can, he attends Bible study and fellowships with other Christians. He displays a high level of Christian maturity that would shame most of us to tears.

Although Andy can speak and make himself understood most of the time, stress has been known to render him speechless. One day an attendant put him on a city bus with instructions to get off at a medical center on the other side of town. Unfortunately, the attendant put him on the wrong bus. Andy soon found himself at the downtown terminal, trying to make a transfer.

Unfamiliar with the bus routes, he again wound up on the wrong bus. He went to the end of the line, had to come back, and eventually, four hours late, reached the doctor's office. The office was by then closed, and he had to wait another two hours for another bus to come along and take him back to the nursing facility.

Most of us have never experienced this man's helplessness and the resultant fear of being stranded. Getting on and off of a bus with a wheelchair is no easy task. Only his faithful Companion Jesus got him through that horrendous experience without an emotional crisis. As panic and fear began to invade his thinking, Andy recognized what was going on and called on the Lord. Instantly, "the peace of God, which passes all understanding" [Philippians 4:7] brought him the stability he needed, and he was able to articulate his problem and get back to the nursing home.

At the height of his panic, Andy made the right decision: He chose to trust God. By not succumbing to his fears, he received spiritual power to deal with his situation effectively.

The world is full of quiet heroes like Andy. Unassuming people, who are generally overlooked, they travel life's journey, often unaware of the profound effect their faithful witness has on others. To the Andys of this world: *Well done, good and faithful servants!* In your presence, fellowship takes on a whole new meaning.

We can only make wise and effective choices when we choose to see and accept reality as it is. Acceptance of "what is" helps us focus on how best to deal with our situation. This frees us to solve problems and issues in ways that work and improve the situation, not add to our pain.

Acceptance frees us to choose. It removes inner conflict that prevents us from focusing on the real issues. Only by releasing our situation to the Lord can we recognize what can or cannot be changed. As we gain discernment, we move with greater freedom beyond the problem. This happens as we place our burden on the Lord and relinquish our fears and our worries, knowing He has the situation under control.

This new confidence then frees us to go on with life, leaving behind defeat and sorrow, indeed, "every sin that does so easily beset us." [Hebrews 12:1] We become *free!*

Imagine your life as a rack of billiard balls, broken apart and fragmented by the impact of a cue ball. The trauma has a shattering effect, with balls (the pieces of your life) rolling helter-skelter, without rhyme or reason, all over the table. The unity and order of that rack of balls has been utterly destroyed. It cannot be put back together precisely as it was before the moment of impact. And yet the game must go on.

Human beings have been created with a built-in resilience

that is made to withstand trauma. Along with a natural affinity for attracting trouble, we are fortunate, indeed, that God has endowed us with this ability to rebuild and reshape our destiny. **What empowers us to do so is our faith in Christ.** We regain control over our lives when we relinquish ourselves to His sovereign rule.

Our empowerment is set into motion the moment we choose not to be dominated by the sickness that is so much a part of the First Order thinking described in my book, *Power to Change*. The only way a battered wife frees herself from an abusive marital relationship, for instance, is because she evaluates the facts, recognizes and rejects the perpetrator's lies that devalue and undermine her sense of self-worth. Thus, the perpetrator's power is broken, and the captive spirit is set free!

Worry cripples and saps our strength.

Faith frees us to act, and in doing so, we open ourselves to a whole new realm of possibilities.

Keep these two diametrically opposed principles, worry and faith, in mind as we meet Megan, a young woman in her early twenties.

When I first met Megan, everything about her demeanor made me think of a whipped puppy. Megan seemed an overly sensitive, though earnest Christian, as she sat in a corner looking on, while others talked assertively around her. Her long straight hair hung down on either side of an expressionless face; she was outwardly attractive, but every line in her face and body "drooped," conveying a sense of hopelessness and quiet despair.

I had the feeling she was a very unhappy individual, and that "believing in Jesus" had brought her very little joy.

Over the next few months, we met from time to time in various social settings. When I finally learned her story, I realized I had not even begun to fathom the pain this young woman was in, or the inner demons that were working so feverishly to destroy not only what was left of her self-confidence, but any hope for her future.

All I knew at the time was that Megan had met and set her cap for an amiable young man, college-educated like herself and a Christian. They seemed well suited, and I was happy for them. After all, what could be better than for two Christians to meet and marry?

After these two dated for about a year, they married, and before long an infant son came along. Amidst the joy that accompanied this new arrival, however, Megan's world came crashing down. Even while she was caught up in the wonder of loving her tiny new son and her own role as a parent, she began to question her own existence and a lifetime of rejection by her own parents. Hugging her tiny son, she wondered, *How could anyone not love their child? What's wrong with me, that my own parents could never love me?* Almost immediately she began to suffer from debilitating migraines and an overwhelming sense of hopelessness.

At times, she was unable even to raise her head from her pillow. Her husband Aaron patiently stayed home for two weeks, then arranged with family members to drop by and lend a hand with the baby until Megan got back on her feet.

Meanwhile Megan struggled along, sleepless and trying to care for a new baby and contending with a growing sense of despondency. Resenting the fact that she felt so helpless and fearing deep-down that perhaps she was unfit. In other words, she had fallen into the pit of lies and distorted thinking that Satan loves to inflict upon God's children when they're at their lowest ebb.

This went on for some months. Aaron hung in there, kept his mouth shut, when he wasn't trying to bolster Megan's faltering faith in herself. Nevertheless, Megan was caught in a downward spiral of depression and seemed helpless to fight her way free. Her depression left her exhausted all the time, yet her obstetrician found no physical deficiencies. Physically, she looked in great shape, having regained her svelte figure soon after delivery. Still, the problems persisted and escalated.

When her baby was nearly a year old, she and Aaron hit a crisis point. They knew their marriage was in serious danger; things could not go on as they were. Fortunately, they didn't fall into the trap of playing Critic, but instead, contacted a trained therapist, a woman whose work I esteem highly.

From the outset, Megan's courage must be commended for facing her problem, painful as the process was. She never tried to whitewash the seriousness of her condition. While she expressed a strong desire to build a wholesome, long-lasting relationship and to create a life for herself wholly unlike the degrading nightmare she had kept secret for so many years, she had a lot of hard work ahead of her before healing could take place.

Before their marriage, Aaron had a sketchy idea that Megan's family was "eccentric" and uncaring, but never realized just how bad things were until she began to undergo therapy. Here, in part, is what Megan had kept hidden for many years:

"I was an abused and neglected child. I was sexually abused by two different people at different times in my life. I was raised in a home that was never clean and where even my smallest physical and emotional needs were not met.

"Most of my childhood memories involve embarrassment and shame, as I was sent to school with dirty clothes and hair and had to endure the teasing and harassment of the other students. I spent much of my time trying to survive on the most basic level and pretending that everything was fine. I never received the nurturing I needed.

"I accepted Jesus as my Savior...at the age of eleven, but because...I wasn't important enough to have my most basic physical or emotional needs taken care of, I also felt I wasn't important enough for God to really love me. I carried such an overwhelming burden of shame and no self-esteem that I couldn't accept God's love. But He loved me anyway, and even though I wasn't aware of it, I now understand that Jesus was with me during my childhood. In fact, I believe He carried me through all the pain...

"Something began to happen to me after [my son] was born. All of the shame and pain I had spent so much time and energy hiding began to surface, and I became a different person than before we were married. I was miserable and depressed, and our...marriage was struggling and slipping away. After a year and a half of marriage, I finally broke down and told [my husband] about my abuse. For the first time, I revealed my horrible secret.

"There was no instant peace or solution to the pain or the confusion I felt. But God began to work in my life and led me to people who helped me understand the pain and taught me to love myself. He led me to a wonderful Christian counselor, put many loving brothers and sisters in Christ in my life, and blessed me with a support group. Most of all, He had already given me a husband who was extremely supportive and accepting."

Megan goes on to share one of the turning points in her therapy: "One of the first verses I was led to was John 1:12-13, 'Yet to all who received Him, to those who believed in His name, He gave the right to become Children of God--children born not to natural descent, nor of human decision, or a husband's will, but born of God.' When I read that verse, God opened my heart, and for the first time I understood that it didn't matter what kind of childhood I'd had, or who my earthly parents were. What mattered was that I had accepted Jesus as my Savior, and ultimately *God* is my Father, and *He* is the One who put me on this earth. On that day, I was able to go one step further and not only accept Jesus as my Savior, but also accept Him as the Lord of my life. [Since then]...the peace in my heart has grown stronger and stronger...God has given me the strength and forgiveness I needed to be able to forgive my parents and the others who abused me, and He has transformed me into a completely new person.

"Through Jesus I have learned to deny the shame that was placed on me as a child and to accept God's love, forgiveness and peace."

Megan's problem is not unusual among those who have been victimized by others. In her helplessness, she had come to view herself as somehow responsible and to blame for the abuse and shame she suffered at the hands of others. Her counselor helped her to see her true worth and to get over the fear that "if people only knew," they couldn't love and accept her. Part of her still longs for her parents' love and approval, but she has come to realize that her own self-worth isn't dependent upon how others view her.

As her therapy progressed, I occasionally bumped into Megan and Aaron. Megan's appearance gradually took on a new glow of self-esteem and an inner peace and beauty. She began to wear brighter colors, and often has a happy smile on her lips. That harried look has been replaced by a growing confidence.

Megan continues to find acceptance and understanding among other emotionally abused individuals in her support group. Recently she became a group leader, and Megan has also expressed the hope that some day she will be able to resume her education and earn a counseling degree. I have no doubt that she will, and that Aaron will give her the backing and encouragement she needs to see that dream to fruition.

You see, dreams really *do* come true when we stop worrying about how others might react if they *really* know us. Like Megan, we need to trust God to do a transforming work of grace and forgiveness in our lives.

Chapter 6. Tough Lessons on Denial

E.   The Tyranny of Avoiding Pain, vs. The Freedom of Choosing to Live *through* Our Pain

By far, the greatest impediment to healing therapies lies in the area of denial and avoidance. This applies not only to recognizing that there *is* a problem that must be dealt with but also to the impact that problem is having on a person's life and on others who may be involved.

Unfortunately, avoidance of pain is the driving force behind addiction, which we covered in the chapter on Erroneous Expectations. This belief system tries in every way not to accept pain as part of life's reality.

Addictive personalities, in avoiding one kind of pain, actually seek out and create more pain for themselves and others; through their addictions, they punish themselves and everyone around them. The aim of any addiction, whether it's substance abuse, sexual, co-dependency, gambling, or any other compulsive behavior, is the temporary avoidance and reduction of the pain of living.

However, avoidance only creates more intense pain and perpetuates the problem. The pain created by avoidance itself becomes an even greater tyranny, holding us captive and cutting us off the possibility of freedom. When we don't face our pain, we become its slave, and a slave to fear, which is at the root of every addiction.

The very nature of pain is a fearful thing. Everything within us militates against it. Physical pain can be excruciating, beyond our human endurance to bear, at times so intense that it actually snuffs out physical life. When pain is present, we cannot ignore or escape it. Its presence compels us to take steps to seek help and healing, and for this much, at least, we can be thankful.

The problem of pain is interwoven with the fabric of living. The negligence and incompetence of others inflict pain. Our own human limitations, vulnerabilities and pride bring about or create pain. Some people are born with severe handicaps, physical or intellectual infirmities that limit or severely restrict, confine and frustrate in ways those who are not similarly afflicted cannot even begin to imagine.

Several years ago, I was making the rounds as a relief chaplain at the Long Beach V.A. Hospital. My duties included visiting new patients, ministering to families, and bringing a word of encouragement wherever I could, especially to those with long term disabilities.

The most difficult wards to visit housed paraplegic and quadriplegic veterans of the Vietnam War. These were men cut down in their prime, bodies mangled by mortar fire, legs and arms amputated, hopes shattered. They had lost everything; many abandoned by family and friends. Hopeless. Nothing to live for. That was my own very human response when I first stepped into one of these wards.

Each of these wards housed twenty-five patients. Paraplegics in wheelchairs moved about in gloomy silence. No smiles, no laughter; just silence. A cloud of depression hung over these unsung heroes.

The quadriplegics were in even worse shape. There is no adequate way to describe the atmosphere. These weren't even the walking wounded. Destroyed bodies lay flat on their backs on gurneys that moved up and down, helping them breathe. Grown men, stripped of their dignity, as they were spoon fed, diapered, and cared for like infants.

They had a perfect right to be bitter. They *were* bitter. At the time, the news they received from the outside came from television sets suspended from the ceiling, telling them how little their sacrifice meant to the American people. Talk about demoralized and despondent vets! These guys must have felt they were at the bottom of the dirt pile.

I used to dread going into these wards. Until one day, when I finished making the rounds of all the other wards assigned to me, and I walked into a ward I had never visited before. That was the day I met Tom. He changed my outlook forever.

Tom was a big strapping black man. A quadriplegic. In plain terms, he had no arms or legs. His motorized gurney moved up and down, keeping all the essential systems in his body moving and circulating.

The first time I saw him, Tom was lying face down on a gurney. His body had been severely maimed. But what I noticed about him was not his helplessness. What immediately struck me was his vital interest in everything going on around him. His cheerful demeanor drew me like a magnet. I noticed other patients kept making their way to his bedside on carts and in wheelchairs to receive counsel from him. When they left, their faces radiated with a peace and joy that men in the other wards didn't have. In his utter helplessness, Tom had a ministry. He ministered to me that day, and I am forever in his debt.

Prior to being drafted, Tom told me, he had been a star tackle on his college football team. He was a fierce competitor who loved to sack the quarterback and tackle running backs. In the Army he quickly emerged as a leader and became platoon sergeant, leading his men through some fierce fighting.

The night he was wounded, his platoon was pinned down and encountered heavy mortar fire. Several pieces of shrapnel were embedded in his spinal cord, leaving him paralyzed from the head down. Confined to a gurney for life, he was dependent on others to meet all his physical needs.

Tom's parents were Christians. Church going and practicing the Christian faith were a way of life for his family. Like many young people, he had partied and dabbled in drugs and alcohol. As Tom struggled to overcome his anger and resentment toward everyone—especially toward God, he grew extremely bitter. Why had this happened to him? He wanted answers that made sense. In desperation, he asked family members and friends to read the Bible to him.

The turning point came when someone read him the Scripture passage where the apostle Paul prayed three times that the Lord would remove his affliction. The Lord's answer impacted Tom like a thunderbolt: "My grace is sufficient for you, for my power is made perfect in weakness." [II Corinthians 12:9]

Then Tom embraced Paul's response to the Lord: "I will boast all the more gladly about my weakness, so that Christ's power may rest on me. That is why for Christ's sake I delight in weakness, insults, hardships, persecution, difficulties. For when I am weak, then I am strong." [v.10]

Tom went on to share his decision to embrace Paul's words as his own. He experienced the reality and power of Paul's words, "For when I am weak, then I am strong." [v.10]

He acknowledged that God permitted his affliction and that he had experienced joy and power in ministering to the men in his ward, many of whom had found their way to Christ through his witness.

He also readily admitted with a twinkle in his eye his human frailty. "Chaplain, I'm no saint walking on water. I have bad moments every day. The pain and frustration of being confined to this gurney becomes unbearable at times.

"Don't get me wrong," he told me. "I'd like to be able to get around the way you do, but since I can't, I've come to accept that God has put me here for a purpose. He spared my life in Vietnam, and He's all I've got. All I need I've found in

Him, and I'm not going to let Him down by grumbling. This is my pulpit, for as long as He wants me here."

Talk about victory! This young man had a battle on his hands, just maintaining.. Yet he radiated more life and more love and more healing power than all his attendants combined.

Despite his circumstances, Tom chose to trust God, and in making that choice, unleashed the power of God to touch other lives. Only one paraplegic ward radiated such hope and optimism. Tom, wherever you are, I salute you, brother!

We could spend a lifetime asking, *"Why?"* Why does tragedy strike? Why must there be so much pain and heartache? We can ask, but that question never provides a satisfactory answer. There are some things that just *are*. We only find the grace to deal with our pain when we stop moaning and accept that life is not always fair, that life has pain, and that we might as well face it and get on with living.

Instead of trying to fix the unfixable, we need to choose how we're going to deal with the reality of "what *is*." Because if we don't, we will only become bitter and invite more pain and suffering into our lives. Deliverance is not found in a bottle, or a pill, or in any other form of avoidance. It is found in choosing to accept.

Acceptance is not passive resignation. Rather, it *activates* our faith and our ability to *choose* and to *act*. It's a choice each of us must make, based upon fact and reality. It does not waste time and energy in obsessive, compulsive behaviors, or distractions. It faces what is going on squarely and deals with the challenge.

The person trying to avoid pain may do it consciously, as often happens in the case of a spouse who refuses to see his/her mate's pain or take it seriously. More often, I find denial takes a more subtle form, arising out of a misreading of the facts surrounding the situation, refusing to see its immediate impact and future ramifications.

In cases like this, a lot of "filters" are applied in an attempt to make life the way it "ought to be, not the way it really is. This inability to face the truth of our situation is like using a theater klieg light to create a totally different atmosphere or interpretation of life through the use of filters that range in emotional tone from black to white and every shade in between. It may look good, but it isn't reality! Moreover, it prevents or delays healing.

Usually this type of denial is employed as part of a defense mechanism instilled in the individual at a very early age. It's survival equipment we use to cope with life. "Fight or flight" is a familiar phrase that describes one of these coping mechanisms.

Denial and avoidance come from deep within our psychological and spiritual make-up. It has to do with our prideful self-image, what the Greeks call *hubris*, which cannot deal with our flawed human nature. Part of our defense against our temporal nature and vulnerability asserts that we should be exempt from misfortune and pain.

Most of us can smile at the gallows humor contained in the statement, "Death is for other people; in my case, God will make an exception." We not only recognize this as denial and avoidance; we see it as wishful thinking. Of course, few of us actually *believe* we're going to get out of this world alive, but we like to joke about it.

Essentially, each of us wants to believe we're exempt, the exception; that we won't suffer the consequences for our actions; that if we do thus and so, life will treat us well.

I'm not saying there's anything wrong with adopting a "positive frame of mind." It makes life easier not to be confronted continually by our own mortality and vulnerability. We want to be in control; we feel we *must* be in control. We just don't want too many unsettling surprises.

That's why we devise elaborate game plans to cover the major areas of vulnerability. We acquire property, set up investment plans and annuities, take out insurance policies, and do everything we can to guarantee success and financial security. When something goes contrary to plan, the structure we have so carefully set up to buttress us against life's storms is rocked and shaken. We begin to question and doubt ourselves in the midst of any intrusive turbulence. We feel our values—at times, our very lives—threatened. Extinction is the great underlying fear, even when precipitated by a lesser crisis.

It is human nature to fear change, which is an inevitable part of any catastrophe or major disturbance of the system of supports we have erected. It's as if our castle is under siege. The enemy of our peace is scaling the emotional walls of our lives. Our first reaction is to go on the defensive, to block the invasion of doubt and fear. We raise the drawbridge and take refuge within the walls. Outside, the sounds of impending battle clamor and beat in upon us. The noise is intimidating, our adrenalin pumps, the central nervous system sounds the alarm.

This is a picture of what happens when the shock of awareness of our true condition first takes over our consciousness. And this is where we generally get into trouble. We compensate by trying to avoid conflict and pain.

As most history buffs realize, there isn't a man-made castle that is impenetrable. Our lives are the same way. Find one vulnerable spot in our defenses, and we are overrun by the horde. What we must take with us into the battles of life, great or small, are the *weapons of the spirit*.

The vulnerability of operating in the flesh instead of the Spirit is a frequent theme of the apostle Paul's. "Within ourselves there dwells no good thing." [Romans 718]

"Not that we are sufficient of ourselves...but our sufficiency is in God" [II Corinthians 3:5] goes hand in hand with his admonition in Ephesians to "put on the full armor of God, that you may be able to withstand in the evil day, and having done all, to *stand*." [Ephesians 6:13] Notice the emphasis on stand; it conveys the idea of stopping the enemy dead in its tracks, of being an impenetrable presence in the midst of danger. Ezekiel also speaks of standing in the gap, thus preventing the enemy's advance. [Ezekiel 22:30]

In my Preface, one of the concerns I address this matter of preventing unnecessary additional damage from occurring following the initial impact or crisis. Damage control. Sparing yourself and loved ones from as much unnecessary grief as possible by not compounding the problem. This can only be done by facing the pain and employing the weapons of the spirit [Ephesians 6:10-18]. It is a complete impossibility, as long as the elements of avoidance and denial are operative in our flesh. Avoidance only compounds and prolongs the healing process.

Back in the early sixties, while ministering in a number of clinical and church settings, I came across an astonishingly brave woman, named after Deborah in the Bible. The name suited her, perhaps because both she and this Israeli judge relied so heavily on God's strength to win their battles.

Debby was a tiny vivacious woman. She was active in children's ministries of the church my family and I attended, and so it wasn't long before my wife and I and our four children became acquainted with her three.

As I soon discovered, Debby had in the span of a year "lost" twin sons. Both had been stricken with a rare blood disorder, the death of the second coming only a few months after the first. There was evidently a genetic component, or so the doctors thought at the time. At any rate, these two little boys died within seven or eight months of each other.

So Debby had started out with five children, three now surviving when I met her.

During the first twin's medical crisis—an overwhelming ordeal for her and the family—her husband Albert decided he couldn't handle any more tragedy. When the second child began to manifest identical symptoms, he ran off with a woman in the church they attended in the San Fernando Valley. Six weeks residency in Las Vegas freed him very neatly from a hurting wife and children, whereupon he and Yolanda, once his wife's close friend, married and moved to San Diego.

He had made his choice—avoidance—a decision that emanated from the flesh and fear and faithlessness.

Meanwhile, Debby was left with three needy school age children and one dying three-year-old. People at church, while not approving of her husband's actions, looked askance, making her feel as if she had somehow failed as a wife, or Al would never have left his family. [This frequently happens where the wronged party, or victim, gets dumped on and is made to feel guilty and unworthy.]

Somehow Debby fought her way through the dark, lonely days that followed. She cared for her dying child, saw the other three off to school every day and made them do their homework. Leaving them with a sitter, she got a job as a convenience store clerk on the graveyard shift to support them.

In those days, there were no health insurance benefits. Wages were abysmally low. Al had taken the car, so she either took the bus or walked. Occasionally some good soul from the women's mission circle dropped by to relieve her, so she could get some rest. But basically she was on her own.

Today Debby recalls, "I just did what had to be done" —a modest understatement. "Sometimes I was so tired, I could barely put one foot in front of the other. But we got by. The kids and I ate lots of chili and rice and puffed cereal, because they were cheap and plentiful."

What Debby doesn't mention is that she suffered terribly from varicose veins and swollen feet, due to standing long hours on cement behind the counter. She doesn't mention the time a robber held a gun to her head, demanding all the cash from her register at two a.m. She doesn't mention stopping by after work to place flowers on her babies' graves.

What she talks about are the funny family experiences that brightened her day. She beams with pride, as she tells about her children's successes in school and later in the business world. She and her children triumphed over heart-breaking times and somehow managed to keep a sense of humor.

But that's not where the story ends. Debby went on to accomplish even greater things after her children were grown. Despite all the demands on her time, Debby had pursued knowledge her entire adult life. The love she lavished on her family spilled over on everyone around her. Seeing the plight of others at work around her, she persuaded her pastor to let her teach literacy classes at church during the week to people who couldn't read.

Soon word of her enthusiasm and effective teaching came to the attention of a local community college, which asked her to teach English as a second language to foreign students. Still the demand for her skills grew. Finally she rented space in a shopping center in a high crime poverty area. She asked the Laubach organization to provide guidance and materials, and not only took on more students herself, but spent time recruiting and training other volunteer teachers.

Over the years, she has helped hundreds of people rise above their circumstances. God led her, step by step, healing her broken heart, strengthening her emotionally and spiritually, and through it all, equipping her for a special ministry to this world's walking wounded.

Now in her sixties, Debby motivates and inspires love and hope in people who might otherwise be dismissed without a second thought. She creates value and esteem among the rejects of society, in those who have given up on themselves.

Years ago, Debby made a conscious choice not to view herself as a victim, but as an overcomer. In the midst of her pain and suffering, she cried out to God and He touched her, changing her life forever. She is an ordinary woman, with one important difference: She knows what it means to tap into the power and the glory of God. The adventure goes on!

Chapter 7. Breaking Free

F. Sick Is "Normal," vs. Healthy Oddballs

The tyrannies pictured thus far are the "normal" responses of those traveling the broad way. Other tyrannies encountered on the broad way include holding on, or insisting on trying to maintain the status quo. People in survival spend tremendous energy maintaining what is familiar, though sick and painful, to them. This tenacious adhering to the old ways emanates from anxiety and fear.

Oddly enough, when God begins to do a work, and life's misery begins to subside and life actually becomes more bearable and even joyous, many people experience a renewed sense of anxiety and even panic. To reduce their anxiety, they allow themselves to become overwhelmed by false guilt, that somehow they don't deserve this sense of wellbeing, and thus they begin to sabotage their own changes for success.

I must caution that this is not a conscious choice, but subtly done. But the moment one becomes aware of this destructive pattern, it is important to recognize that the author of all lies, deceptions and human misery, *i.e.*, the devil himself, is fighting to regain control.

I have seen this pattern repeated in numerous cases. Yet, if we recognize what is going on, we can apply the Scriptural injunction, "Resist the devil, and he will flee from you" [James 4:7], with good effect.

Our human make-up is so vulnerable! Our innately addictive, sinful nature gravitates toward destruction and resists embracing healthy life experiences, which come about by the exercise of our faith in God. Faith threatens and militates against continuing on as we were and are. The instant we become "new creatures in Christ," the tug of war between our two natures begins.

To give control to God means to transfer our allegiance; it means ceasing to rely upon our own limited creaturely resources. It means placing ourselves fully at the center of God's sovereign will. This goes against the grain of our pride, which lies at the root of every effort at self-reliance, which is not to be confused with entrepreneurial self-help, or moving out in faith. What is at issue here is whether we are operating in the flesh or in the power of the Holy Spirit.

Nor am I for an instant encouraging unhealthy co-dependency upon others. What I *am* emphasizing is the absolute necessity of **unconditional surrender to the will of God.** This voluntary giving up of the controls of our life requires turning our backs on the destructive forces (still present) that have robbed us time and again of the inner freedom we crave with all our heart, mind and soul. This is our spiritual birthright, ours to claim from time immemorial. This freedom becomes ours the instant we choose Christ and become His children and heirs to the kingdom.

This is not hypothetical hot air. This is fact! Transformation, or conversion, is the saving process whereby God rescues us. If you recall the movies, *Backdraft* and *Towering Inferno*, you have a fair picture of the urgency of our need, and how God, in His infinite mercy, hauls us from the burning building of our captive mindsets and poisonous habits and envelops us in the pure oxygenated healing of His love.

We are set free! Free from the smothering wreckage of the old life. We cannot save ourselves, except by casting ourselves into the safety net of God's love. He catches us. He changes us. He empowers us.

So you see, there is **power in letting go**. As each of us comes to see the bankruptcy of our human condition and resources, we stop playing around. We stop trying to play God.

A person tyrannized by holding on is like the man trying to get through an airport loaded down with a dozen pieces of luggage. He drops one bag, tries to retrieve, and drops three more. A porter comes along, but he refuses help. Then, just as he almost has everything balanced, he pitches forward on his face.

My own wife tried this stunt recently in the Chicago Amtrak station and took a terrible fall down an escalator. Although she claims the worst blow was to her pride, she wound up badly hurt and out of commission for the remainder of our cross-country trip. Rest assured, she *will* use a porter next time!

Many of us are like the foot soldier trying to slog his way through the desert sand during the Gulf War. Thinking to make it easier on himself, he straps himself to a tank, only to discover this heavy vehicle had trouble maintaining traction. Soon he is buried up to his neck in sand! We, too, become buried by life's experiences, unless we choose to unstrap ourselves and cast our burdens upon Christ.

There is a story about a woman in China, walking down the road with a heavy pack on her back. A man driving an ox cart stopped and offered her a ride, which she gratefully accepted. As the ox carried them along, the driver invited the woman to unstrap her pack and let it rest in the back of his cart. His passenger refused, saying that since the driver had been so gracious as to offer her a ride, she could not possibly let him carry her pack as well. Of course, we see the absurdity of this reasoning, but how many of us are in God's "cart," just barely, but still insist on traveling the distance in our own strength?

Blessed is the person who becomes so tired of carrying his burden, that he/she stops carrying unnecessary baggage!

The freedom of letting go comes only when we relinquish life's baggage and hold a funeral for all that dead weight. Travelers on the narrow road travel light. They discard baggage from the past, lest they become weighed down.

The broad way is strewn with people struggling with unnecessary burdens or sunk in holes created by tanks spinning uselessly in the shifting sands of life. Travelers on the broad way use a tankful of gas to go nowhere, while the narrow road traveler gets a hundred miles to the gallon. It doesn't take a genius to figure out why broad road travelers end up exhausted and depleted by the journey.

The Tyranny of Giving Control to Others:

Many people spend their lives looking for experts to assume responsibility and to take care of them. Political, religious, business and educational leaders are among the many experts on the broad way, promising much but delivering little or nothing—certainly nothing of eternal value. Multitudes on the broad road are encouraged to "go along with the program," and not to think or do for themselves. Considering the high casualty rate of many government programs, the cost has been horrendous to provide social and educational programs that have, by and large, failed to do what they promised. Our highly subsidized broad ways are strewn with fatalities, individuals who no longer can think or choose, while the experts prosper and tighten the noose of their control. And all the while, individuals suffer and social conditions worsen.

Travelers on the narrow road are empowered by an intimate knowledge of their Savior and by the fact that Christ's atonement on the Cross has restored their personal worth in His sight. These people have **power to choose** and **freedom to reshape** their own destinies under His direction. As they depend on God for their life, power and wisdom, they are no longer dependent upon the whim of power-hungry "traffic cops" along the broad way.

The Tyranny of Outward Form:

Travelers on the broad way are obsessively concerned with how they appear to other fellow travelers. Consequently they lie to one another, seeking to deceive and make others believe they are not what they really are. Travelers on the broad way are always covering up their flaws. They live in constant fear and anxiety that they will be unacceptable, if their true condition is ever found out.

Some time after World War II, a man returned to his home town, and let it be bandied about that he had been wounded and decorated for heroism during his tour of duty. He also claimed to have earned several college degrees. Based on this representation, his community helped elect him to Congress. At first, his charade worked, as he manipulated and went to extreme measures to keep from being found out. When he was finally unmasked as a fraud, he was forced to resign and drifted into obscurity. For a while, he had gained the whole world, but eventually lost everything, including the love and respect he so desperately sought.

As travelers on the narrow road, we need not strive for such attention. We need not be encumbered. Narrow road travelers admit their vulnerabilities; they accept their clumsiness; they also keep choosing the empowerment of God, rather than the accolades and hand-outs of men. These travelers grow in grace, as they progress along life's way.

The Tyranny of Feelings:

A great deal of energy is expended to reinforces the notion that life should always "feel good." To many people, this seems a plausible life goal, to surround themselves with an environment that will maximize our comforts and minimize our pain. In fact, it sounds like what God originally designed for our wellbeing in the Garden. The problem is, when we become gods unto ourselves, we automatically set in motion what became an integral part of the human experience after the Fall of Man. As a result, reaching this goal becomes a debilitating obsession for the broad road traveler.

The obsession obscures the reality that all human feeling is a response to our imperfect perceptions of the world. Trying to capture and maintain good feelings encourages a denial of reality; it further distorts the beliefs that govern our lives and produces painful and destructive patterns, which eventually cause breakdown and immobilization.

I have observed and sometimes treated people caught up in always having to be "up" and "positive" and sunny, regardless of how life really is under the spit and polish we present to others. One such lady, a beautiful woman who seemed outwardly to lead a charmed life, was always in perpetual motion, caring for the needs of others. She was always a ray of sunshine to her large following, who hung on her every word at the weekly Bible studies she taught.

Yet there was much beneath the surface that was *not* happy, and she refused to acknowledge or see it. Eventually she collapsed under the strain. She spent the next two years getting herself back together physically and emotionally and spiritually. She was an "on-fire-for-Jesus" Christian, but she was addicted to always having to feel good. Where she got into trouble was in not listening to her Lord, and being afraid to acknowledge her humanness. She was surrounded by other Christians in her ministry, but never able to let down her hair and let others share closeness.

This pretense and denial had its origins in the "old life" and may have been what prevented her marriage from being as rich as it could have been. At any rate, the Lord, while never ceasing to love this willful child of God, allowed her to struggle with this bit of erroneous thinking until she surrendered it. I am happy to relate that she now has a much better grasp on what really matters. She is back on track and more of a blessing to others than ever.

Freedom In Knowing the Truth:

Travelers on the narrow road seek to walk in intimacy with our Companion Jesus. To do this, we must submit ourselves to being governed by the truth and genuineness that are inherent in the character of God. Travelers learn every nuance of His character, until eventually our focus and thinking become one with His.

Our confidence level grows with every step taken, until we can say with the Psalmist, "Even though I walk through the valley of the shadow of death, I will fear no evil, for Thou art with me." [Psalm 23:4] Our paths become so inseparable that even when that Final Curtain falls on this temporal scene, we experience no separation from our faithful Life Companion.

This Companion is our Great Shepherd, Jesus, who "makes us lie down in green pastures." He leads us unerringly beside the "still waters" and along "paths of righteousness." He removes inner turmoil and restores within us His mind and His truth.

Our Shepherd provides for our wants and our needs. His companions enjoy a spiritual feast in His presence, while enemies seeking to divert us to the broad way look on in envy. He singles us out and anoints us, providing such an abundant outpouring of His Spirit that we can face any threat encountered along the checkered confusion of intersecting broad ways that zig and zag across our narrow path.

Our confidence grows with each encounter and each victory, so that we no longer have any desire to experiment or dabble in the world, but follow on, knowing He has provided a glorious mansion, just suited to our individual needs and tastes, where we will sit at His feet and worship Him continually.

What certainty we have in Christ! What freedom!

Another of the benefits of knowing the truth about ourselves is that it helps us refute the lies and prejudices of others. Many of us can relate to Rosa Parks, whose tired aching feet launched the desegregation of buses in Montgomery, Alabama in 1955. Here was a woman who had all her life been subjected to the slurs of racial hatred. She had suffered greatly, because of the injustices imposed upon her people. All her life, she had put up with unfair laws and rules inflicted by white supremists. All her life she had sat or stood at the back of the bus in the area designated for black people.

The burden of lies and distorted thinking heaped upon generations of blacks was no light thing to take. For those who have never encountered the capricious and militant social climate of the South in the first half of this century, it is difficult to imagine what a sore affliction this treatment must have been to those living under its domination.

But this lady chose not to believe the lies that sought to "keep her in her place" and make her out to be less than the courageous woman she was. She may not have reasoned it all out, but she knew, deep down inside, that she was as worthy of respect as anyone else who lived and worked in that city—in the nation, for that matter. She was a child of God, and that entitled her to some respect!

The day she stepped on the bus, paid her fare, and sat down in a seat reserved for white passengers, Rosa Parks became the catalyst that launched the civil rights movement and changed American history forever.

All because her feet hurt, and she was dog-tired.

She didn't set out to change the system. She was merely asking for the same consideration as any other paying bus patron. Of course, when Rosa Parks refused to give up her seat and move behind the color line, where there were no seats available, she was arrested. This resulted in a boycott by black people refusing to ride the city transit. Many bus passengers were black, and eventually economic pressures forced the city fathers to yield.

Meanwhile, the movement of civil disobedience spread. Whites and blacks from all over the country jumped on the band wagon, participating in boycotts and sit-ins and demonstrations. And thus began the breakdown of social discrimination in the South and elsewhere.

Discrimination started to erode and lose its power when black people exercised their collective power and chose to get drastic. This is clearly one of the best defined examples of a spiritual warfare and what happens when people refuse to accept the lies and distorted thinking of those in power.

As long as the city fathers and the bus company continued to impose their distorted, devaluing policy on their customers, it was necessary for people like Rosa Parks and the many thousands of people enmassed under the spiritual leadership of Dr. Martin Luther King to take a stand. There was bloodshed; there was heartache; there was sacrifice. But there was also victory, because they were willing to pay the price to support a righteous cause.

Rosa Parks' life demonstrates that travelers *do* get their feet trampled and hurt, but as they persevere along the narrow way, as they evaluate the truth and refuse to be intimidated by those traveling the broad way, in time they find rest for their feet.

Our steps may falter and appear clumsy at times, but we *will* get through the dance of life. A few years ago during a PBS-TV tribute to Fred Astaire, Ginger Rogers described the filming of a particularly grueling dance routine, which, if I recall correctly, involved dancing up and down an elegant staircase and around a stately ballroom.

Always a perfectionist, Fred insisted on rehearsing for hours. The final "take" was shot at three in the morning when Ginger's feet were swollen and in excruciating pain.

The interviewer commented that he would never have guessed the dance wasn't the work of totally spontaneous inspiration. Ginger Rogers responded that throughout her long career, dancing had always remained her great joy. Even when pain was present, it couldn't diminish the joy of the dance.

So it is with those traveling the narrow way. Pain is part of the price for our freedom and our joy.

The broad way is strewn with those who have rejected the disciplines of the Master Choreographer and turned a deaf ear to His direction. Many cease to dance because their feet hurt, or the musical tempo coming at them is a bit too demanding, or they see a particularly difficult combination step coming up. Instead, they head for the nearest rest stop, where they try not to distress themselves unduly by becoming involved in the pain and suffering of fellow travelers.

Meanwhile, Jesus, our Companion on the narrow road, continually takes us aside to wash our dirty, scuffed feet and apply the balm of comfort and healing. Often He shares with us the task of washing each others' feet, of offering the solace only another weary foot soldier or traveler can comprehend and respond to. He is right there throughout the journey, from start to finish..

"Lo, I am with you always." [Matthew 28:20]

Coming up!

Section Two will touch the hearts of anyone who has lost a child. The story of Vicky demonstrates the spiritual freedom my wife and I experienced, as Christ helped us get through the trauma of losing her so unexpectedly. To God belongs all the credit, for it was done *not* in our own strength, but in the power of God!

Section Two. POWER TO CHOOSE

The Death of Our Baby

Vicky

by Barbara Dan

"A little angel came, smiled, and turned around."
—Scandinavian Proverb

Introduction

Our fourth child, Victoria Marie Dan, died in her sixth month of life, struck down by what is commonly called SIDS (Sudden Infant Death Syndrome). This phantom virus claims the lives of over 25,000 infants every year in the United States alone. No one knows who this tragedy will touch next, or when. It is no respecter of persons, visiting affluent as well as poor and middle income families.

What these parents share in common is their grief and sense of isolation and bewilderment. Often their grief is compounded by having to deal with the criticism of outsiders, who don't have any more idea what happened than the parents do. Because so few seem to understand SIDS, surviving family members are frequently left to handle their grief the best they can.

SIDS is not a modern medical mystery. The dispute brought to Solomon in I Kings 3:16-28 may well have involved a SIDS death. While one woman accused her companion of killing her child by rolling on him in her sleep, there is no real proof of that. In fact, she didn't know anything was amiss until she awoke in the morning to nurse her son and discovered the other woman had (allegedly) switched babies.

From the Bible and other ancient writings, we know that grieving parents and surviving family members have been trying to make sense out of this tragic occurrence since the dawn of history. The effects often have long term, destructive impact upon the family unit.

None of us ever realizes how great our spiritual resources are until we are called upon to test God's provisions during times of extreme difficulty, sorrow and shock. Like many people, I had never really allowed myself to trust God touching the matter of how I would react and deal with death. Consequently, I was totally unprepared for God's power, which was abundantly supplied when our lively, seemingly healthy baby died suddenly during the early morning hours of Tuesday, August 2, 1966.

The account that follows was written only a few weeks after John and I experienced our loss. Since then, I have had time to reflect and evaluate the impact of this trauma and our own family's recovery. What we learned and lived holds true today, as much as then. I hope, through reading our family's story, other parents will receive some comfort and come to see that you can face life's trials and sorrows without fear.

Lovingly,

Barbara Dan

God is our refuge and strength, a very present help in time of trouble." [Psalm 46:1]

Where It All Began...

This is the story of how our saucy, dark-haired little daughter, Victoria Marie, with her laughing eyes and warm happy ways, transformed our family's lives forever. And how she became God's instrument, teaching us some of life's richest and most difficult lessons.

Vicky burst onto the scene in the wee hours on the morning of January 4, 1966. I can still remember how cold it was during that rushed predawn trip to the hospital. My husband John and I barely made it. What a hurry Vicky was in to make herself part of our family! Between hard contractions, I made a mad dash from the parking lot to the lobby, where I was promptly taken upstairs. Vicky was so busy being born that I couldn't get onto the gurney in the hall without help, or sign my name properly on the permission forms. I was rushed through double doors straight into delivery, and a few minutes later met our third daughter, Vicky, a perfectly formed, robust infant, 8 lbs. 3 oz., 20-1/2 inches long. God's little Christmas present to the Dan family, although she arrived a few days past her due date.

From that moment on, I can safely say there was never a "typical" day in our household. Our three other children, Georgia, Carrie and Michael, were all close in age and constantly under foot, being too young for school, and a certain amount of routine had to be maintained to care for our four lively preschoolers and also preserve the parents' sanity! Without some organization, how *does* a mother manage simultaneously to feed two little ones in diapers! I can still picture myself at the table at mealtime, Vicky consuming a bottle on my lap, Michael, only twenty months old, being fed from my left hand, while the two older girls, four-and-a-half and three-and-a-half, were supervised on my right. I know no better way to acquire administrative skills than trying to juggle the needs of four little ones, all close in age, all vying for Mom's attention at the same time!

Every new day became an adventure in our tiny two-bedroom apartment. A lively polka down the center of the living room; sailing boats in the bathtub; building tents with quilts and "camping out" between two bureaus in the bedroom; or praying over a hurt finger were just a few of the children's varied pastimes.

Our home—"central headquarters"—was so crowded with baby paraphernalia that I jokingly referred to our menagerie as "wall-to-wall babies"!

That wacky first month, Vicky guzzled everything we gave her and never slept more than two hours at a time.

John was chaplain at the Salvation Army's vocational rehab center in Van Nuys, California, and going to school, so we were pretty exhausted by our little lambchop's voracious appetite for formula. Fortunately, a woman in John's office, who had cared for over three hundred foster babies, advised us to slip dehydrated banana flakes and cereal into some of her bottles.

Right away, our chowhound settled into a less frantic, more enjoyable period of her life with us. She enjoyed her food and was the best eater of the four. She liked to play games and would grinningly collect food in her cheeks, then drool it down her chin. What an impish laugh, when I'd try to shovel it all back in! If she was wearing a dress, that usually got shoved into her mouth along with her food by a wee fist.

I used to sing to her constantly while spooning in the baby food. Her excited, happy response soon prompted her to attempt to sing along in wordless, high pitched squeals of delight. We could hardly wait for her to join Carrie, Georgia and Michael in the simple children's choruses. She soon earned the nickname "Vicky-bird," for she would wave and flap her arms excitedly to accompany herself.

Our little "zoo," I soon wrote my mother, was made up of Georgia the mule, Carrie the possum, Michael the monkey, and Vicky-bird. I don't think any family could have felt more blessed.

Despite all the attention lavished on her, it always seemed remarkable to us that she never became spoiled or demanding. She received and was so responsive. But she retained a sweetness and gentleness that must surely be reserved for those angels who are earth's visitors only for a short time.

I'll never forget how delighted and thrilled Georgia and Carrie were with Vicky the first time we decked her out in a tiny dress for church. We scotch-taped a tiny red and white bow on her head as a finishing touch!

Right from the beginning Vicky was in on everything. At three-and-a-half months, she camped overnight with us at Lake Cachuma, where Georgia encountered a fierce wild goose in the women's restroom and came squawking [Georgia, that is] across the field at top speed, the irate goose beating at her with its enormous wingspread!!

From five months of age on, she would swing her legs and bounce on my lap, grab the pages of our Bible story book and try to cram the book in her mouth. She would look over her shoulder at me and laugh with those wonderful brown eyes.

Vicky went with us to vacation Bible school, shopping, the zoo, a wedding, parks, and the beach. On our last excursion to the beach, she ate her first marshmallow. She looked like such a merry imp with bits of it stuck to her tiny nose and hands. I cuddled her down near the water, while John ran along the water's edge with Georgia. Carrie and Michael spent their energies knocking down a magnificent sand castle.

July Fourth marked Vicky's sixth month "birthday." Joking, I told the children that the President of the United States had declared a national holiday to celebrate Vicky's being six months old.

The Salvation Army where John worked had several events planned that day, and we spent most of the day at the rehab center with the men and the Major in charge. While I was in the kitchen chatting with the Major's wife, Vicky chomped ecstatically on my thumb. Suddenly she bit down particularly hard, and I felt her first baby tooth sink in. Georgia and Carrie insisted on feeling it, too. Both of them cheered and clapped over this "first" in Vicky's life.

In July she also went with us to the local swimming pool. When she became tired and fussy, a mother of three, who had recently lost her fourth child, offered to rock her to sleep for me, while I kept an eye on our rambunctious son, Michael. Countless children were drawn to our baby that day. She had a quality of spirit that just beckoned. After a brief nap, she came into the pool with me and showed off to all her young admirers how well she could kick and splash. She thoroughly enjoyed herself and never showed fear of anything, except Michael when he occasionally overdid one of his embraces.

In mid-July she attended a missionary potluck at church and managed to capture everyone's attention with her high pitched singing and arms outstretched to everyone within conversational reach.

Sunday, July 31, was Georgia's fifth birthday, a very important event in Georgia's life. The night before, I made thirty-four cupcakes and frosted them with pink, blue and green icing at 11:00 P.M., then put them carefully away where Georgia wouldn't find them. We went to church Sunday morning, knowing that shortly after lunch, a crowd of children would arrive to surprise our excitable Georgia.

Most of the children came to Sunday school and church with us—nine in all, with Michael the only boy, poor dear! After delivering sermons for the Salvation Army, John planned to come by the church to pick up the children and me. After the service, I situated myself and all of Vicky's gear under a pine tree in front of the church and fed her a bottle. It was quite hot, and the breezes seemed to refresh her.

Meanwhile the other children raced inside for iced tea, with Michael bringing up the rear. His comical swagger and aggressiveness made me laugh as I cradled Vicky on my lap. Her eyes laughed up at me. She was so responsive to my every thought and mood.

After lunch, the children came to Georgia's party. Georgia was so thrilled and surprised. I played games with the children, including London Bridge and Pin-the-Tail-on-the-Donkey outside in the 100° heat, while John tinkered with a broken phonograph, which he repaired just in time for Musical Chairs. The children certainly polished off those cupcakes in a hurry, too!

Fortunately, Vicky and Michael slept through the worst of the heat. They awoke at four after everyone was gone, and after a bite to eat, we drove to a friend's home in Burbank to pick up a loveseat I planned to reupholster. John squawked good naturedly about his extravagant wife who purchased such sturdy, well built loveseats for $5!

We took it home, then went to view "The Paul Carlson Story," a film about the martyred Belgian Congo missionary doctor, at another church in the San Fernando Valley. The testimony of Paul Carlson's life and witness among those he served made a profound impression. Upon our return home, we put the children to bed and turned in fairly early ourselves.

Monday, August 1. I drove John to his office in Van Nuys. Then I hustled our uproarious smallfry over to the public health center, where Carrie and I had tetanus boosters, and Vicky received her third oral polio immunization.

Returning to our apartment, I put Vicky down for her morning nap. The landlady contacted me about 10:30 A.M. to let me know that a three-bedroom apartment was available in the building next to ours. It was downstairs, freshly painted, ready for us to move into.

I was delighted, because we were about to burst the seams in our two-bedroom apartment. John and I had been sleeping on a hideabed in the living room. Michael and Vicky shared one bedroom, while Carrie and Georgia shared the other. Vicky's bathinette, bouncy chair, walker, playpen, high chair and infant seat took up a good part of the living room and kitchen.

Two-year-old Michael and Vicky were a cheery, chirpy pair in the bedroom we had relinquished to them. Every morning we heard their sweet voices, as they greeted each other through the bars of their cribs. Georgia and Carrie, despite occasional clashes, had converted their little bedroom into a schoolroom, into which they ushered Michael on a fairly regular basis as their prize pupil.

The three older children ministered with me to Vicky, and she returned so much love, enthusiasm, mischief and laughter that we felt God had sent us a little part of Himself. Even when a day didn't turn out quite the way we hoped, or some disappointment in John's work was felt, Vicky and our other children always brought us a sense of joy and deep satisfaction.

When I inspected the new apartment that Monday morning, I found it freshly painted, but the floors were a mess. After lunch, I took Vicky and Georgia over with me, while I washed the floors. It was almost unbearably hot, as I scrubbed and scraped an incredible amount of dirt off the floor tiles.

In the heat, Vicky soon became extremely restless. Two neighboring children, Sheila and Helen, tagged along with Georgia and me, playing with Vicky and trying to cheer her up. I brought her playpen over from home, and she seemed more content, although she cried a lot just as I finished up.

Then home for a bath. Vicky seemed to want to be held more than usual, but soon was laughing as much as always that late afternoon. I thought perhaps her polio immunization and the soaring temperatures must have contributed to her discomfort. Her bath seemed to perk her up, however. How she loved to kick her feet and laugh and splash in her little blue bathtub!

After she ate—lightly, because of the heat—I put her down for a late afternoon nap.

After an early supper, I piled the children into our GMC Suburban Carry-all and went to pick up John and two men from the Center who had volunteered to help us move. On the way home, Vicky kept getting on her hands and knees in her car bed and laughing at us. John turned around at almost every stoplight to see his "little Petunia" frisking. As Georgia later remarked, "Vicky was sent from God to teach us all laughter." How true that was!

We got home around 6:30 P.M., and by 8:30 P.M. most of the larger items of furniture and beds were moved over to the new apartment. Michael even helped me tote some small items. I recall humorously that one of our new neighbors importantly pointed out to another family, "Reverend Dan and his family are moving in."

How his face fell as Michael came around the corner, bare-bottomed, carrying his diapers in his hand!

Right behind him, I looked like a lean Russian wolfhound just back from a swim in a river; my hair and clothes were dripping and plastered to me with perspiration.

Only Vicky, bouncing along merrily on my hip, managed to look fresh in the heat. I remember thinking that we were certainly making a great impression for the Lord!

Oh, well, I thought, harkening back to when I was a professional actress before my conversion to Christ, *I can't always look like something out of a fashion magazine.* (Truthfully I rarely did with four preschoolers to keep up with!)

About 7:30 P.M., Carrie, Vicky and I went to the grocery

store to buy soft drinks for everyone, because it was so hot. Vicky rode on my hip, hanging over my arm slightly, waving and chirping to Carrie, who trailed a few steps behind. Vicky made even the ordinary seem special, and even though I'd been working hard physically all day, I felt full of energy.

At 8:00, I put Vicky and the other children to bed. The girls were unusually cooperative about getting on their nighties. Carrie even laid out Georgia's nightgown for her, which struck me as being so thoughtful. I fed our squirmy little Vicky a bottle on the couch, while she played with a toy. Because of the heat, I put her to bed, wearing only a diaper, rubber pants, and a thin cotton top.

She seemed restless and didn't want to go to sleep, but she laughed over the end of her crib and bobbed her little head up and down in her funny way as she bounced a bit. Two days before, she had begun getting up on all fours. She was the picture of health and happiness at 8:30 P.M., when she dropped off to sleep.

After John returned the men to the Center, he and I continued to straighten things up. I lined kitchen shelves with paper, worked hard and long on the bathroom, then showered and cleaned up a bit.

Close to midnight, we were still going strong. We planned to move the smaller household effects over in the morning before John went to work, so we called it a day. As always, we both went in to check on the children before retiring.

Every night I told the children that the Lord was watching over them and loved them, for I am certain they can hear even in their sleep. Vicky was quite restless and tossing in her sleep. Because of the unrelenting heat, we didn't put any additional clothing on her. I settled her down on her tummy, kissed her soft baby hair and patted her as I told her, "Jesus loves you, Vicky."

Little did I know that would be the last time I would see

her alive.

Pleased with our spacious new quarters, John and I retreated to our bedroom and read from the apostle Paul's letter to the Philippian church. The verse that made the greatest impression that night as we talked was:

"...that I may know Christ and the power of His resurrection and the fellowship of His sufferings..." [Philippians 3:10]

Then my eyes dropped down to Philippians 4:13 and 4:19, heavily underlined in my Bible, where Paul wrote, out of his deep experience with Christ:

"I can do all things through Christ who strengthens me...My God shall supply all your needs according to his riches in glory by Christ Jesus."

We prayed, turned out the light and went to sleep, never dreaming what an impact those verses were about to make on our lives.

Tuesday morning, August 2, 1966, our world turned upside down.

We awoke about 6:45 A.M. when Georgia came into our bedroom, dressed in her sunsuit. Beaming, she told us she had even made her bed.

The other children had not awakened, so we jumped into some old clothes hurriedly. The phone and gas weren't connected in our new apartment yet, and I was just about to go out the door to prepare French toast in our old apartment across the way when Georgia went into the bedroom Michael and Vicky shared.

She exclaimed in a puzzled tone, "Mommy? Daddy! Vicky is hanging."

We thought Vicky must be kicking her feet through the crib rails, so we dropped everything and rushed to greet our little cherub.

Somehow Vicky had gotten wedged between the rails and

crib springs. She was hanging by the neck, pale and lifeless, her feet dangling several inches off the floor.

"I think she's dead, John," I breathed, as we moved quickly toward her.

John reached her first, and it took a tremendous effort to free her. We threw aside the springs and mattress, and John lifted Vicky out. She had swallowed her tongue. John quickly cleared an airway and began mouth-to-mouth resuscitation, even as we carried her between us to the living room couch.

I dashed outside to a fireman neighbor, because I remembered he had rescue experience. He was on duty. However, my shouts roused several neighbors. One man came and helped John try to revive Vicky, while someone else called the Fire Rescue Squad. I grabbed John's car keys, thinking we should drive to the nearest hospital emergency room, but then realized I was in no shape to drive that distance and the Fire Rescue would undoubtedly reach us first.

I came back inside the apartment momentarily, hardly able to pray or think. We rubbed her little legs, trying to warm them, and got a quilt for her. John was sobbing between breaths as he tried to get her to breathe. I went back out to the front curb, thinking the Fire Rescue would never arrive.

Finally they showed up. They came in without any equipment at all. As they examined Vicky's cold little body, I saw a tiny bruise on her chin where she had hung from the crib. The Fire Rescue team could do nothing. When I asked it they shouldn't try to jump-start her heart with electric paddles, they said it was too late. Then they asked, matter-of-factly, but at the time it seemed so cruel, what mortuary we preferred.

Preferred! I looked at them, aghast. Hadn't they understood anything? We wanted our baby alive!

I had no answer; neither did John. My mind momentarily froze. Fortunately, John had the presence of mind to go to a neighbor's phone and call Bill, a deacon from our church, who arrived in minutes with his wife Marian. She and I sat together while a policeman came to make out a report.

When the policeman left, he said simply, "I know the Lord is with you." It was a simple enough thing to say, but we already sensed that God was strengthening us. I appreciated his quiet manner and kindness.

Then two detectives came and took pictures of the crib and took another report. Last came a young mortician, representing the coroner's office. He also made a report.

The facts they compiled seemed so cold, so unfeeling. Our baby was six months and twenty-nine days old. In perfect health. We furnished them with the name of her pediatrician and anything else we could think of that might shed light on her death. We knew all of this was standard procedure in cases of accidental death. But when your baby is lying there, and you would give anything to see her little tummy start moving up and down again, it's hard to talk about these things with strangers.

I was numb. It seemed incredible that sometime during the early morning hours, Vicky had cut short her earthly visit and returned to Jesus.

Early that morning, even amidst the initial horror and shock, God began to minister to us in our loss. Scriptures came to mind at precisely the right moment to bolster our anguishing hearts. As I sat looking at our little angel, still lying on the couch, sunken in appearance, wondering where all her rolypoly fat had gone, God sent a measure of peace.

John and I knew she was with Jesus.

A fleeting mental picture of Vicky playing among flowers in a bright patch of sunlight lifted my spirits momentarily beyond the temporal scene of investigative figures wandering through the apartment, transporting me, of all places, into the realm of praise. It wasn't something I conjured up. It came unexpectedly, like the comforting touch of a Friend.

Now, I am as skeptical of "visions" as most twentieth century believers, but I accepted this as God's assurance that my baby was happy and with Him. I received the strong impression that **this death wasn't meant to destroy, but to build our lives and to exalt His Name.**

Because of my strong aversion to death, even the death of one of the children's pet turtles or goldfish, I had convinced myself I could never stand up under the death of a loved one. I was sure I could never survive such a loss. Yet I found myself able to look with peace upon our dear precious baby, who meant more to me at that moment than anyone else on earth.

I knew Vicky had left her earthly tabernacle for a heavenly body which would never be touched by corruption, decay, illness or sin. I was comforted to know she would never experience sorrow or anguish such as mine.

It may seem odd, but I was so *thankful,* in that moment, that Jesus had come to "taste death for every man" [Hebrews 2:9]. What love, that God sent His only Son Jesus to die on our place. What love, that He had given us His full assurance that our little ones are in His safekeeping.

"Let the little children come unto me, for of such is the kingdom of God" [Matthew 19:14; Mark 10:14; Luke 18:6] took on new meaning. I knew without a doubt that God, Who had raised His own Son from the dead, would not fail me in that terrible hour.

We cannot hope to fathom *how* God works in these circumstances, but that He *does* suddenly became a certainty.

The writer of the book of Hebrews reminds us:

"Because the children are partakers of flesh and blood, Jesus also Himself did likewise, that through His own death [on the Cross] He might destroy him that has the power of death, that is, the devil; and *deliver them who through fear of death were all their lifetime subject to bondage.* For truly, He took not on Himself the nature of angels, but He took on Himself the seed of Abraham. In all ways, He was made like [us]...*For in that He Himself has gone through testings, **He is able to sustain those who are tested**.*" [I encourage you to read various translations of Hebrews 2:14-18 for the fullest, richest meaning.]

Because of Christ's work on the Cross and His resurrection, John and I never gave way to a sense of futility, as we faced the fact of Vicky's death. I was able to rest in the knowledge that God would use our Vicky for *His* purposes in death, just as He had in life.

Co-workers from the Salvation Army, church members, neighbors and friends from the Hollywood Christian Group soon began to appear on our doorstep. Each offered to help in different ways, and the final stages of our move from the old apartment began. One dear friend from John's office, who had lost her husband several months before, did our laundry.

I sat there while John left to make phone calls and preliminary arrangements for the funeral. Somehow God was making it possible for me to bear this loss.

Even amidst my tears and pain, I couldn't help thinking of a Jewish girl in the other building, whose baby son was a month older than our Vicky. Her son had been critically ill almost from birth and for some time had been in intensive care. For three months his life had hung in the balance.

For weeks Christian friends and I had prayed for her baby, and God had given his family back a healthy baby boy. God gave me a thankful heart, as I sat across from Vicky's lifeless form. I was so glad this neighboring family had been spared the sorrow of separation from their little one. For I knew, without the knowledge of Christ's resurrection power to sustain me, I would have been in a state of collapse, bitterness and abject despair.

After all the necessary reports were taken care of,

someone took me out for a brief walk, so they could remove Vicky's body, her belongings and the crib.

Almost immediately I met the Jewish girl from the other building. I spoke briefly to her about my hope in Christ and how glad I was that God had spared her son. Truly, God had prepared my heart in the moments prior to our meeting, to show her the love of Christ.

When we returned to the apartment, Vicky's things were gone. Oh, how my heart ached. The apartment seemed so empty without her! I remembered how warm and happy she had been, snuggling up against me the evening before on our way to the store.

Neighbors and friends from the church came and helped with the everyday tasks that had to be done. A neighbor woman took our other children to her apartment for breakfast.

Meanwhile, some dear friends propelled John and me into a car and took us to the most dismal breakfast of our lives. I am not a calendar watcher, but when I saw the big "August 2" over the cash register in the restaurant, my heart cried out within me. Food just didn't taste like food, however; even liquids were difficult to force down.

John and I wept freely, and our Christian friends were wonderful in their efforts to lend support and comfort. Although we felt like Job, we didn't have a single one of Job's "friends" to add to our heartache. How we thank God for sending just the right people to us that day!

Returning home from breakfast, we took our children aside and told them simply that Vicky had gone to heaven that morning. They didn't seem the least bit upset. To them, it seemed the most natural thing in the world for her to be with Jesus.

Five-year-old Georgia was happy for Vicky and volunteered, "Jesus has given her a new body." I remember how we laughed at the idea that she would have a full set of teeth the next time we saw her in heaven. Then the children went outdoors and enjoyed splashing in a plastic wading pool most of the day.

We were surrounded by friends, all encouraging us to verbalize our grief and our faith. They helped us keep moving through the day, sharing the many tasks that are so necessary in caring for a family.

Little children who had gone with our family to vacation Bible school that summer came and silently put their arms around me. With great simplicity of faith, our children told their little friends that Vicky was with Jesus in heaven, and that she had a new body like His.

Nearly a hundred families in the housing project were challenged to think about spiritual matters. A few small children made cruel remarks, which only reflected their parents' lack of understanding and compassion. By God's grace, I was able to speak lovingly to them without allowing their words to turn us bitter.

Then toward evening, the next door neighbor, a man we had never met, moved out, lock, stock and barrel! I don't know whether Vicky's death, or the manner in which we were dealing with it, was something so alien that he couldn't handle it. It hurt a little, but God's Spirit buoyed us up throughout the entire day.

Despite the mortician's urging, we didn't try to be brave, only *believing*. We claimed God's promise: *"All things work together for good to them that love God and are called according to His purpose."* [Romans 8:28]

We wept with our friends, but through it all, the hope Jesus plants in the hearts of His children shone through and made people realize that God does truly undergird and sustain.

Many people came by to share with us their past griefs and the victories God had won in their lives.

One such visitor was an Olympic diving champion's wife,

whom we'd known during our acting careers. Together we rejoiced again over the way their three-year-old had literally been recalled from death a year before. He had choked on a tiny piece of carrot and stopped breathing. His sister ran to a neighbor for help, while his mother started mouth-to-mouth resuscitation. Finally the paramedics came. After three hours of resuscitation, little Paul regained consciousness.

His mother recalled praying continually, "Thank you, Lord, for the time we've had Paul with us," as she worked to revive him. She never thought he could be brought back. Yet God is wonderful in His love. His plans cannot be frustrated, and so He gave them back their little son, as healthy and whole as ever.

I couldn't help thinking of Hebrews 11:35, as she told me her experience. "By faith women received their dead raised to life again; and others were tortured, not accepting deliverance, that they might receive a *better* resurrection."

Missionary friends from India dropped their plans and came to help me finish moving the last of our things from the old apartment. Together we folded laundry, cleaned and put things away. Coral Baker, whose own daughter had seizures after a fall down a steep staircase caused a concussion, refused to let me berate myself for putting Vicky to bed in the crib. She made me realize the destructiveness of blaming, or laboring over thoughts of "if only" and "what if..."

A former nightclub performer came over and delighted our children with games. Georgia, Carrie and Michael were enthralled by his loving personality and antics. They had a grand time playing with Johnny.

A young woman, married to a blind pianist, told us how she was pronounced dead as a young girl, after an intoxicated physician prescribed the wrong medication for her. After making funeral arrangements, her Christian mother, unable to believe it was God's will for her young daughter to die, had prayed. God answered by raising her daughter up again, to the utter astonishment of the doctors and mortician!

Another couple from John's office shared how their baby had died early in their marriage. How bitter they were, until finally, broken and empty, they turned to God and began to understand that their baby was safe with Jesus, and that their little one was God's instrument, bringing them to Himself.

Our pastor's wife, Winnie, came and prepared dinner, then bathed the children. She and her family knew what it was to lose a baby; they had given a seven-month-old son back to the Lord many years before.

Our church moderator, an older man whose magic tricks had delighted the children at vacation Bible school, shared how he had lost two children, and how God had used his little ones to deepen his own walk with God.

As we listened, John and I began to see a pattern emerge. Often the very young, so special to God, are able to lead others into the kingdom of God, when all else has failed to move the parents.

Later that night, we learned that our fireman friend, who had been on duty that morning, had fallen over a cliff while fighting a brush fire in the hills. His life was saved by hanging onto the hose in his hands.

We were again reminded how, two weeks before, John had rushed another of our neighbors to the hospital in the middle of the night. The man would have died if he hadn't had emergency surgery; God wasn't ready to call him home yet. Again, we sensed the hand of God.

All these things which were shared with us pointed to God's perfect timing. **God never allowed anything to come into a person's life that He doesn't also supply the capacity and the ability to deal with the situation.**

Of *course*, we would have preferred God to spare Vicky. But we didn't dispute His wisdom.

After all our friends had finally left, the longest, most heart-rending night of our lives began. As soon as we were alone, we tried to get the children to sleep. They also felt Vicky's absence more keenly once their playmates and friends had gone home.

As we sat in the semi-gloom of their room, glad the dim light hid our tears, we spoke to them about our beloved Victoria Marie.

Georgia and Michael finally dropped off to sleep. Carrie, not quite four, didn't fare so well; she cried periodically through the night. Finally, clasping a soft doggie she had shared with Vicky to her chest, she slept.

That night we discovered that Vicky was helping Carrie realize how important she is to us, also. As I tried to console her, Carrie looked up at me with big sad eyes and said, "It's not so important to be the first, is it, Mommy?"

Suddenly I understood: Carrie had a new self-esteem. She had been our temperamental one, a fiercely competitive rival of her sister Georgia, who is a year older. All our efforts to ease the friction between them had been to no avail during for nearly two years—until Vicky's birth.

From the time we learned Michael was about to become a happy addition to our family, until Vicky's conception, Carrie proved hard to handle. She would kick out windows, bite, fly into tantrums for no apparent reason.

But when Vicky was on the way, her outbursts stopped as suddenly as they had begun . Carrie would "hug" Vicky in my tummy, and that little life came to mean a great deal to her, even before we had a formal introduction. Always competing, Carrie prayed "against" Georgia for a baby sister. How thrilled she was when our Christmas present from the Lord turned out to be a baby girl!

Carrie was especially helpful in fetching and carrying for Vicky. We were a team. Even Michael took Vicky's wet diapers gingerly into the bathroom for me. All the children took turns "babysitting" for the few seconds I would turn Vicky over to them while I got a bottle, a jar of baby food, or clothing for her.

After the children finally slept that first night following Vicky's death, John and I walked from room to room, talking. We gazed out Vicky's bedroom window at the darkened heavens, discovering in some small measure what that dark hour at Gethsemane must have been like.

We tried to rest, but all we could see was our precious Vicky hanging from her crib, and the Son of God hanging on that Cross. Some may call it coincidence, but we found God drawing us into a deep fellowship with the sufferings of Christ. We felt the impact of Mary's sorrow and were in awe. How much it must have cost God the Father to send His only Son Jesus to the Cross for a lost and dying world!

In my pacing that night, I came across a church bulletin from a boys' reform school where John had preached during July. The Beatitudes were printed on the cover, and my eyes fell on Jesus' words: "Blessed are the pure in heart, for they shall see God." [Matthew 5:8]

How that described our Vicky!

And now she was "face to face with Him in all His glory," as the hymn puts it. Even so, I was deeply troubled by the way in which she had gone to be with Him.

Then the Lord seemed to speak to me from His Word: *"Cast all your anxieties on Him, for He cares for you."* [I Peter 5:7]

"Come unto me, all you who are weary and heavy laden, and I will give you rest. Take my yoke upon you, and learn of Me, for I am meek and lowly in heart: and you shall find rest in your souls. For My yoke is easy, and My burden is light." [Matthew 11:28-30]

"Trust in the Lord with all your heart; and lean not unto your own understanding. In all your ways, acknowledge Him, and He shall direct your paths." [Proverbs 3:5-6]

At the point of our greatest need, God met us—again—and sustained.

We couldn't hold back the floodgates on our tears; we didn't try. Some well meaning friends had suggested a sedative to help us through the first few days, but we cast ourselves completely on God, trusting Him alone to see us through. We knew that giving expression to grief is healthier than a "stiff upper lip." We were not embarrassed or afraid to let our emotions go.

Never in the long terrible hours that followed were we alone, for God was with us. Paul, in II Corinthians 4:8-9, could have been describing our experience when he wrote of his own hard life: "We are perplexed, but not in despair...cast down, but not destroyed."

In I Corinthians 10:13, God gave further assurance that "there is no temptation [or testing] come to you, but such as is common to man: but **God is faithful** and will not allow you to suffer above what you can stand, but will...provide a way for you to bear it." By releasing ourselves to His care, we found God supplying a strength that far surpassed our own puny strength; the supporting arms of Jesus gathered us close and got us through.

That night we also read John 11:1-46, the account where Jesus raised his friend Lazarus, already dead four days, from the grave. How our hearts burned within us! We dared to pray that God might raise our Vicky up off that cold mortuary slab. *Please, God!* How we longed to hear the telephone ring during those early morning hours. If only the mortician would call and tell us to come get our Vicky, who was alive again and craving a bottle. *Oh, God, we know you can do it. Please make the phone ring.*

But the phone did not ring. Only in our minds and hearts.

There has never been any doubt in our minds that God has the power to breathe life back into our loved ones, even after death. After all, He created this magnificent universe. He has dominion and power over all His creation. "All things are possible with God." [Matthew 19:26; Mark 10:27] But we also recognized that Vicky would still have this mortal body; even if she *were* resurrected, she would have to undergo physical death again.

Then, too, Lazarus's resurrection didn't convince everyone to have faith in the Lord; not everyone who beheld his resurrection chose to believe. [John 11:46-47] Perhaps more could be accomplished in death with all its starkness. Still, my heart yearned to have Vicky restored to us.

Finally, in the stillness of prayerful listening, Jesus' words came, gentle but insistent: "Forbid her not to come to me, for of such is the kingdom of God." [Mark 10:14; Luke 18:16]

We knew then that we must give her back to God in our hearts, relinquishing *everything* to Him. With Him, Vicky would have a spiritual body, not subject to death and all that this world knows of suffering.

As we examined the highly personal meaning of her life and death, John and I found a new dimension to our love emerging, as we encouraged each other to express our grief and our faith. A handclasp or an arm around the shoulder took on new tenderness. There sprang up between us an unspoken understanding that was communicated without words. This unexpected bond drew us even closer together in our marriage.

As l paced the floor that night, my mind went back over the past several months. I was so *thankful* for all the time I had spent playing with Vicky, enjoying and caring for her, and holding her on my lap each evening while I read Bible stories to the other children. All these memories and many others to the other children. All these memories and many others flashed through my mind during that long dark night of sorrow.

The circumstances surrounding Vicky's death strongly tempted us to blame ourselves for somehow failing to prevent such a tragedy. We had always "babyproofed" our home. We were very conscious of safety factors, keeping medicines and potentially dangerous products well out of reach. It wasn't difficult to believe we had failed our baby.

Even as I review the events years later, it seems impossible that Vicky could have gotten stuck between the crib rails and the rigid bed springs that supported her mattress. She was a good sized baby, over eighteen pounds at the time of her death. The crib had seemed safe and sturdy when we placed her in it the last night of her life.

Even so, she was dead.

It would have been so easy to heap condemnation on ourselves for placing her in that crib. *Why, in the rush to get settled in, hadn't I thought to put her in the net playpen? Maybe then she would still be with us.* These were the kinds of questions going through our minds.

The next day a dear friend told us the hardware on her son's brand new crib was slightly loose like Vicky's, yet he slept in it without incident from birth until he was nearly three years of age.

Three other Christian friends told us their little ones had become trapped in their bedding, despite perfectly firm crib rails. Fortunately in all three instances, the mishap occurred during the day, and the parents walked in at the crucial moment to rescue their infants. These dear friends will never realize how comforting it was to hear their experiences, for the picture of our baby hanging from that crib was etched vividly in our minds for weeks following Vicky's death.

My own mother told John how she had put me down in the middle of a double bed when I was only eight or nine pounds, using a chair propped against the side of the bed to prevent any danger. A few minutes later, she came in from outdoors to find me hanging through the chair slats screaming. She could never understand how such a small infant managed to scoot three feet and get tangled between the slats. From discussions with other parents, I became aware how many infants had close calls, even with the most conscientious parents.

It became apparent that we couldn't allow bitterness to invade our home. It would be destructive to relationships and cut us off from the loving presence of God and His resources, which we needed so desperately! It would mar sweet memories of our fellowship as a family and cast a shadow over our love for Vicky.

Convinced that God's will could *only* be to uphold each other through this difficult time, John and I dared not allow false guilt and doubts to invade and destroy our confidence in Christ.

God meant Vicky's death for good, a truth that seemed as potent as when Jacob's favored son Joseph voiced it to those same brothers who had sold him into slavery. [Genesis 45:1-8] While God had not caused her death, we began to see that He could bring much good out of this terrible tragedy.

Thursday morning, August 4. Vicky would have been seven months old today.

Two-year-old Michael awoke before 5:00 A.M., calling, "Vicky 'wake, Mommy? Vicky 'wake?" This was his usual morning call, and oh, how we wished it were so! When he refused to go back to sleep, we got him up and played with him in the living room. He did his best to divert us from sorrow and was most demonstrative and charming, as he pranced about, chattering animatedly.

A short time later, Georgia came in and smilingly told us she'd had a dream. "Vicky was playing and being so silly,

Mommy. Throwing books and toys around and laughing and crawling." Of course, our baby hadn't begun to crawl yet, but it seemed to us that God had sent this dream to Georgia to comfort us all.

Our four-year-old nature lover, Carrie continually brought in dandelions, wild flowers and bits of flowering shrub to us during the day. We were glad to have the children share with us, and we did what we could to encourage them, rather than isolate ourselves from them in our grief. We knew they, too, needed to express their love for Vicky.

Much of my time prior to the funeral was spent sharing what God communicated moment by moment to my heart. I felt as though God was truly walking and talking with me from His Word. Constantly He upheld me, keeping the channels of faith and love open, so that I wouldn't withdraw into myself but use this opportunity to comfort and strengthen those around me. [God deserves *all* the credit for my being able to testify so freely, for I am ordinarily not that outgoing.]

At first, I hesitated to go view Vicky's remains. When I saw her later that afternoon, my initial reaction was that this couldn't be Vicky's little body. She didn't look like herself at all. She was dressed in a lovely white dress I'd never seen before and wore tiny white shoes. Her hair was brushed back neatly. So unlike our tousled, barefoot baby! I wanted to muss her hair.

As I stood looking down at her in that tiny casket, I knew with absolute certainty that Vicky had gone to be with the Lord, but I found comfort, too, in the reverential, loving manner in which her body had been prepared for burial. We had cared for her so tenderly in life, and to have others share in her care, even in death, helped. It also helped ease the pain of discovering her hanging from her crib. We asked to have her hair brushed into soft bangs so she'd look more like the Vicky we had known.

Much of what I had once ignorantly condemned as pagan, such as making up the remains and so forth, struck me now as being actually quite kind to the bereaved. It is right to handle a person's body reverently after death. That tiny body was once occupied by a living soul.

As we left the mortuary, I laughed for the first time since her death at some recalled whimsical action of Vicky's.

That night I went over to a Hebrew-Christian girl friend's apartment nearby to type up the order of service for the funeral. Eileen and I talked at length and yet with a lighter heart, as together we rejoiced in our common faith in the historical Jesus and in His resurrection, upon which rests the entire Christian faith.

By 1:00 A.M., John and I were asleep, finally able to rest peacefully.

Friday, August 5. The day of Vicky's funeral.

Instead of wearing a somber green suit, as previously planned, I chose an orange-red plaid suit, gold shoes and a white hat. My Vicky would not have me grieve in sackcloth and ashes. John wore his best brown suit for his "little Petunia."

As we left for the funeral, I told our children that friends would be coming to lunch afterwards to celebrate Vicky being with Jesus. The teenage daughter of a friend stayed with them.

We arrived long before the church doors were open. Two men from the mortuary were already there with Vicky's casket. Entering the church, I passed the spot under the pine tree where I had fed Vicky after church the previous Sunday. A flood of memories returned. I wept on John's shoulder, but felt peaceful that God's will was being done.

We tape-recorded the service for out-of-town relatives who couldn't be there. We knew Vicky was helping many family members to see God's love more clearly, and we wanted let them share in this time of sorrow and victory with us.

After the service, which featured Easter hymns of celebration and two outstanding sermons, the casket was opened. Although many were shaken and tearful, Christian friends were unafraid and strong. Others, whose lives were still not committed to the Lord, appeared frightened and disturbed in the presence of death. To the lost, death must seem so final. I confess that without a personal knowledge of God's forgiveness and resurrection power, I would have been totally without strength that day.

After others had paid their last respects to our little angel, John and I approached the form of Victoria Marie. John was heartbroken, though not despairing, as he kissed her cold little forehead.

To those standing around us by the casket, I remarked what a beautiful body God had given her to live in, and how I had loved her little hands, lying now so still and lax. She had been such an animated baby, and this unresponsive, solid figure, though sweetly scented and seemingly asleep, was just too small to contain the great spirit we had come to know and love.

I felt calm as the casket was closed for the last time and we went outside to invite our friends to lunch after the graveside committal service.

Vicky was buried at the top of the highest hill in the Forest Lawn Cemetery in Burbank, overlooking San Fernando Valley and Warner Brothers Studios. A brief service of Scriptures and prayer concluded our earthly care of her.

A wave of terrible loneliness and pain swept over us, and we clung to each other in grief. We felt so helpless. It was really difficult to turn and go back to our car, leaving her alone on the hill with a mortician's assistant. When we got to the bottom of the hill, we looked back at the white casket and flowers moving slightly in the breeze. We knew it would be a long time before we saw our precious Vicky again.

♥

We Had Only Just Begun...

When we named our baby Victoria Marie, we had no idea she would live up to her name so beautifully—it means "victorious" and "exalted." She is truly proof in our lives of the victory Christ has won over the grave. She has been exalted to live in His presence forever.

Two days after Vicky's burial, Sunday, August 7, marked a new beginning for John and me. It was like a first century Resurrection Morn as John preached three extemporaneous messages of triumph, first at a Baptist church and then at the Salvation Army alcoholic rehabilitation center, where he served as Chaplain. In the evening service at our home church, I was also privileged to share some of the ways Vicky had already begun to minister to our hearts, deepening our faith and ministry to others.

A full schedule of preaching occupied most of August for John. We both spoke words of encouragement to Christians in churches all over Southern California and as far away as Las Vegas, Nevada.

The next week several young women at our church in North Hollywood began a weekly Bible study. Their interest in spiritual growth was the direct result of seeing the joy and peace we had experienced during our sorrow, and so the Victoria Bible Study Group began to meet every Wednesday morning. In the months that followed, their rededication and growth, prompted by Bible study and obedience to God's leading, had a profound influence in reviving the church's desire for outreach.

Unable to get the picture of Vicky hanging from her crib out of my head, I became concerned about the threat that crib rails and general crib design can pose to a small child. Improvements in crib design and construction could save several hundred babies each year. Yet most parents are unaware of the dangers. I decided that while I couldn't do anything about Vicky's death, I should try to prevent other tragedies.

Soon after the funeral, my children's pediatrician put me in touch with a friend on the local Safety Council. I discussed the need to promote better crib design with a reporter from the *Los Angeles Times* and shared my research. Hoping to avert other tragic crib deaths, I took photographs from various angles of a life-size doll, using Michael's crib to illustrate how easily crib accidents can happen.

I had just put away my camera and flash equipment on the morning of September 8th when Vicky's death certificate came in the mail. I looked it over carefully, never having seen one before. When I came to the Cause of Death, instead of the expected "strangulation on crib rails," or similar terminology, my eyes fell on an unfamiliar and wholly unexpected term, "acute leptomeningitis."

I wondered if there was some kind of mistake. We had experienced many heart-wrenching moments during the month following Vicky's death, wishing we'd put her in her net playpen that night instead of the crib.

I telephoned a nurse friend, who read the medical dictionary's definition of leptomeningitis. It had absolutely nothing to do with strangulation, smothering or asphyxiation, which the mortician had told us was the probable cause of death.

I then called our pediatrician, who got a copy of the coroner's report. We learned that approximately 25,000 infants in the United States die annually from an unidentified and, thus far, unstoppable deadly virus. It hits with all the shocking suddenness of a runaway high speed train. When this phantom virus invades the system of an apparently healthy child, death usually occurs within a very short period of time, sometimes within minutes.

The autopsy revealed that Vicky's lungs, spine and brain were affected by a high fever. She had all the symptoms, we were told, of Sudden Infant Death Syndrome, which has been researched and so widely publicized in recent years.

As John and I discussed this latest revelation, he recalled how Vicky had swallowed her tongue, making resuscitation nearly impossible. Evidently a convulsion had ended her life, and in the throes of it, thrust her body in between the springs and side rails.

Our doctor assured us, as did the public health nurse who came to our home, that Vicky would have died that morning, even if she had been in the hospital, and regardless of the crib she had slept in.

> *"Wait on the Lord; be of good courage,*
> *and He shall strengthen your heart;*
> *wait, I say, on the Lord." [Psalm 27:14]*

We learned an important lesson during that difficult first month: It is best to wait on the Lord and trust that His ways are right. It would have utterly destroyed our marriage if I had blamed John for a loose screw on the crib, or if he had blamed me for wanting to move that day. Dismantling and moving the crib had resulted in loosening its hardware.

At the time of Vicky's death, my first instincts had been correct: It would have accomplished nothing for John to be burdened down with frustration and guilt, because he hadn't been able to secure that one screw with wood putty. It was a small omission but, we had both thought, a fatal one.

Now we realized that in the exercise of forbearance, we had truly covered "a multitude of [imagined] sins" [James 5:20]. *Not*, I hasten to add, by denying the facts, for we were quite open in our conversations with others about this imagined flaw in the crib, but by showing each other compassion instead of a spirit of criticism.

I cannot tell you how relieved we both were, as we read and re-read that autopsy report four weeks later. We still had our marriage intact, our love for each other was stronger, and our other children had come through feeling protected and loved. Such was the grace of God at work in our lives!

After we learned the actual cause, we were even more certain the Lord had not intended us to stand in the way of Vicky's sudden homecoming. He had used her to do a special work of grace in our midst.

ARE WE EVER REALLY PREPARED?

Three months before Vicky's death, a serious viral pneumonia with secondary complications had almost claimed my own life. Now, as we adjusted to our loss of Vicky, I was able to see God's hand in my own illness. My bedside chats with the children about heaven and how death was like walking into another room with God holding our hand, had prepared the children to accept Vicky's sudden homecoming more easily.

Although death comes to all of us unexpectedly, we can prepare ourselves to face whatever life brings, through daily study and prayer, always keeping God's will central in our thinking.

I also view this loss as a clarification of my relationship with the Lord. Absorbed like most mothers with raising a lively young family, and devoting so much energy and love to the task, it is easy to wonder sometimes if we might not be neglecting our service in other areas.

Jesus asked his affectionate but fickle friend Peter, "Do you love me more than these?" After Vicky's death, I was even more certain that Christ did, indeed, come first, for I experienced no bitterness toward God over our loss.

For the first time, I was able to appreciate the significance of the sacrifice Abraham was called upon to make in offering his son Isaac to the Lord. Despite our doubts and heartache, God must have our complete trust and obedience. Our precious children, upon whom we lavish so much care and devotion, so many prayers and hopes, cannot in any way be withheld from God. *He is their God, too!* Our plans for them must not stand in the way of His higher purposes.

CAN WE EVER LOVE TOO MUCH?

I often felt, while Vicky was with us, that perhaps I loved her too much. But my love for God emerged stronger, affirming to me that my devotion to the children and John was never in conflict. Loving my children did not compete with my loyalty to God and His service, but gave tangible expression and proof of my love. This experience has led me into a deeper faith and reliance upon God.

A dean from the Episcopalian seminary in Berkeley, California, once told a gathering of seminary wives, at which I was present, that we should thank God each morning and night for our loved ones and give them back to God each evening. Now I know why. Sometimes we have to learn experientially that *these little ones are not ours at all. They are only on loan from God.*

Of *course*, we want to protect them from harm! That is part of our calling as parents. That's why we mirror His watch-care over us in all that we do for the children He places in our care. But we will never be able to ward off every negative experience or danger. We will never be able to isolate our children from disease, hostile elements of society, or the toils and snares of this life.

What we *can* do is entrust them to God's safekeeping. We can introduce them to the Savior at an early age. We can nurture them spiritually in Christ, for then, regardless of what the future holds, we can have confidence that *"He is able to keep that which we've committed unto Him against that day."* [II Timothy 1:12] With this confidence, even after devastating loss, we can again press forward and live in the sunshine of His love.

It's Okay to Feel Pain.

Part of our problem as parents is our fear of pain. It hurts. We don't like it; we don't understand it; we want it to go away. We don't want any reminders that we are never really in control. All such reminders of our fragile humanity strike us deeply in our pride. If we could, we would deny the existence of grief and pain altogether--and *especially* we would do away with death.

It may ease your heart somewhat to remember that **pain is essential to healing**, whether experienced on a physical, emotional or spiritual level. We shouldn't try to block it out, but work thorugh it.

One of the most vivid illustrations of this truth is found in Dr. Paul Brand's books about his work with lepers in India. Because leprosy attacks the peripheral nerves, lepers lose the sensation of pain and often sustain serious injury to hands, feet and other body parts.

Dr. Brand strongly affirms our need to be thankful for the presence of pain. It tells us something is wrong and impels us to take action and seek healing. This coincides with the adage, *"Earth hath no sorrow that heaven cannot heal."*

Jesus said, "Fear not those who kill the body but are not able to kill the soul; but rather fear the devil, who is able to destroy both soul and body in hell." [Matthew 10:28; Luke 12:4] Jesus also told a prominent religious figure of his time, "You must be born again." [John 3:7] Rebirth or conversion, a turning from sin to God, from darkness to Light, brings about new life, refreshment to the soul, freedom from the weight and burden of sin and despair.

We may still encounter our share of trials and sorrow, but a new principle begins to operate when the Spirit of God indwells us. Like a river of living waters flowing over our mind and spirit, He saves us from stagnation and death.

God really used Vicky to put things in the right perspective.

Sometimes you can't change the outward circumstances, but you *do* have a choice about how you face them. After Vicky, we discovered that we had the **power to choose** how we responded to tragedy. We could let it destroy us, or we could tap into the power of God and experience His life flowing through us.

Standing in the presence of death need not be terrifying. With God at your side, it can be a time for ultimate truth. As our family depended on the Lord, death brought us to the threshold of a glorious new life in Christ.

I would not be completely truthful, if I didn't add that we continued to shed plenty of tears in the months that followed. We experienced a good deal of loneliness for that dear little face. We will never forget her, nor the pain of separation. But we love Vicky too much to grieve selfishly. Her joy in God's presence is so much greater than everything we shared with her here on earth.

SOME LESSONS YOU NEVER FORGET

Isaiah 61:3 promises that God will "give them that mourn...beauty for ashes, the oil of joy for mourning, the garment of praise for the spirit of heaviness; that they might be called trees of righteousness, the planting of the Lord, that He might be glorified."

The truth of this Scripture has been borne out in our experience and in countless lives. As a family, we have walked through troubled waters before and since. We have known joy in times of testing, serious illness and, in this instance, death.

The length of life is not so important in His sight as what that life accomplishes for God. Fruit borne in a tiny life is far better than a long but purposeless existence. "He who would save his life shall lose it," Jesus cautioned, "and he who would lose his life for my sake and the Gospel's shall find it unto life eternal." [Matthew 16:25]

The impact of Vicky's life and death will always be felt. It is impossible to predict all that her dear life will inspire and motivate us to do, but we know without a doubt she has been God's little missionary to us, and to many others over the years.

"Heaven will be like Vicky," Georgia once told me. Every time I hear the Doxology sung in church, "Praise God from whom all blessings flow," I am reminded of Vicky. The phrase, "Praise Him above, ye heavenly host," includes her in that number gathered around God's throne.

Truly her life and death have done more in our lives than the most eloquent sermon ever could. She gave love in ways that were unusual for a baby. It's almost as if she were reinforcing Paul's admonition, "You received; now *go* and give what you have learned and received and heard and seen in me; and the God of peace shall be with you." [Philippians 4:9]

No wonder we felt that Christ had sent a part of Himself, for He said, "Except a kernel of wheat fall into the ground and die, it abides alone; but if it die, it brings forth much fruit." [John 12:24] I am also reminded that, *"A little child shall lead them."* [Isaiah 11:6] and *"Where your treasure is, there will your heart be also."* [Matthew 6:21; Luke 12:34]

Truly, God sends crosses for us to bear, so that we might crucify all pride and gain more completely the mind of Christ. Our reliance upon Christ and our love for Him are deeper because of the way He has ministered to us through the death of our little one. Vicky has seen to it that our family will turn neither to the left nor to the right, but continue on the course which will lead us eventually to His throne. There we shall enjoy fellowship with loved ones and with our Master and Friend, Jesus Christ, who has not left us comfortless.

Even though some of us may bear the cross of sorrow for a long, long time, it will never be too heavy to carry, for we have the resurrection promise: "Christ died for all, that they which live should not henceforth live unto themselves but unto Him who died for them and rose again." [II Corinthians 12:9]

"Lo, I Am with You Always"
[Matthew 28:20]

Looking back, I realize that my feelings and my faith in Christ were always the most true at those times when all I could manage was to cast myself *entirely* upon His grace to see me through. "My grace *is* sufficient." [II Corinthians 12:9]

Here in Las Vegas, where tragedy seems to stalk families and lonely people are often consumed with despair, God has called us to serve Him. This city is probably the last place on earth I would have *ever* chosen to live. But God knows best.

But first He equipped us; *then* He sent us. I praise Him for the scores of families and individuals whose lives are different because of what God privileged us to experience through Vicky's death. I am always mindful that *"We have this treasure in earthen vessels, that the excellency of the power may be of God, and not of ourselves."* [II Corinthians 4:7]

Life-shaping experiences are part of how God equips us to serve others. For how can you comfort others, if you have never known the Comforter's sustaining power and love first-hand? What do you say to a grieving family when their little one lies stiff and cold in the grave? When the toys are all put away and the house is too quiet? When empty arms ache for consolation, and seemingly no one else understands or cares?

The Scriptures are Life and Light for our path in the darkness, but when you can also reassure a grieving Mommy or Daddy from personal experience, their hearts are often opened to the tenderness and saving power of Jesus Christ. **There is a ministry given only to those who have suffered and overcome.**

Many years later, I am even more convinced that there is no adequate answer to be found outside of Jesus Christ.

Section Three. POWER TO CHOOSE:

The Dynamics of Powerful Living in Christ

by

John Dan, M.A., M.Div.

"For when I am weak, then am I strong."
--II Corinthians 12:10

Chapter 8. Spiritual Power in Weakness

One of the great paradoxes of the Christian faith is found in Paul's statement, "When I am weak, then am I strong." [II Corinthians 12:10]

It seems incomprehensible to the finite mind that the most leveling of experiences often launches the human spirit to heights and dimensions of life that were totally beyond comprehension before.

POWER WHEN WEAK? The first response may be, What lunatic nonsense is this? How can this be, when no strength is left, and grief and loss have left us shattered and reeling with disbelief? What mockery is this? When all that is precious is gone, when a love as essential as oxygen is suddenly taken from you, Paul's observation may well seem like the utterance of a madman.

Why should anyone who is suffering heed such a foolish boast?

While I agree that on the surface Paul's statement makes no sense, I must also point out that First Order responses [described in my book, *Power to Change*] are made from outside the realm of faith and spiritual experience.

What lends authenticity to Paul's words is found not in theological or philosophical debate, but in *experiential* Christianity. These are not rash words. The demonstration of God's power is most evident (and less likely to be overlooked) when it comes to us in our weakness, in our moment of greatest vulnerability and pain.

This concept of "strength in weakness" goes contrary to everything we have been taught since the earliest hours of our existence. We have been taught to strive and to fight and to survive. This, incidentally, places us in an adversarial posture with fellow travelers; not a pretty picture, but there you are: slugging it out to maintain your personal "space," to get your fair share, to gain recognition and love from "significant others," *i.e.*, our parents and other occupants of the planet who operate under the same system.

We go on like this, operating in what I describe in my book, **Power to Change**, as the world's First Order System, until we finally figure out that all our wrangling and contriving and striving is actually circular in movement, and we are working awfully hard and getting nowhere fast.

Somewhere along the way, our wanderings are brought up short by what may be likened to a headstrong bird dog jerked up tight on a choke collar so he will heed his trainer's command. Something in our path mercifully brings us to a screeching halt, so God can get our attention. For others, this awareness comes on more gradually, that life isn't quite the bowl of berries we expected it to be, and we're basically pretty empty inside.

However this "revelation" of our condition breaks in upon our consciousness, it is guaranteed to make us think: *What's it all about? Why am I here? Is this all there is? And, if so, why am I never satisfied?* The questions vary, reflecting our spiritual condition and general dissatisfaction with life.

The catalyst that confronts us with the need for choice and change may be a crisis, or it may be some person or challenge God has allowed to cross our life path.

But being human, we instinctively swerve to avoid the path of pain and cost. We will not travel that path, until we have exhausted every other avenue. (I had a hound dog like that once; he would never "come," unless he was boxed in by fences, and then he was the best behaved dog you ever saw!)

This leaning toward avoidance and denial is why it generally takes a crisis or major turning point before we consider Paul's "secret formula" for success.

When we find ourselves utterly cast down, when we reach the outer limits of our own strength, when our hopes and dreams fail, when all our pat answers prove hollow, we finally get around to asking the question, "O wretched person that I am! Who shall deliver me from this deadly existence?" [Romans 7:24]

At this point, we concede the possibility that the answer may actually lie outside of ourselves—indeed, outside the realm of our finite understanding and experience.

Praise God! We are finally on track. It may take a while, but we have taken the first step toward discovering who we are and toward reaching our spiritual destination.

This is often followed by our recognition of who God is and what He has done through His Son to bring us into right standing with him. Providing we seek His forgiveness and intervention, we then receive the gift of conversion, or the "born again" experience.

It has been my observation as a therapist that most conversions are genuine but shallow. This does not invalidate the child's relationship with his heavenly Father; indeed, it is never dependent upon our merit but *solely* upon His grace and the atoning work of Christ on the cross.

However, **the degree to which we yield to the Lordship of Christ is the degree to which we experience the joy of personal transformation.** God in His infinite patience and mercy continues to shape us into His likeness, in order that the "fullness of Christ" might dwell in us and be a part of our experience. [Ephesians 3:19; 4:13]

Paradoxically, this reshaping process usually involves the pain of confronting the truth about ourselves. In doing so, God leads us to recognize the worthlessness of placing any confidence in the "flesh," *i.e.*, in temporal things, and causes us to rely more and more upon the indwelling power of the

Holy Spirit. It is this indwelling presence and power of which Paul makes his boast, and any person seriously interested in dealing more effectively with life's trials owes it to him/herself to examine not only the conditions under which Paul wrote, but the validity of his claims.

Paul was a well educated Jew, well versed in Hellenism as well as the Jewish rabbinical teachings. Born with privileges above most of his peers, Paul was broken of his pride and wonderfully converted to Christ on the Damascus Road, after leading a persecution of those "disruptive" followers of Jesus who persisted in following The Way.

Struck blind, he was led like a helpless child into the city, where he soon revealed his changed heart to some of the disciples, who were skeptical at first. After all, the beloved deacon Stephen had been martyred while this fellow Paul stood by, giving sanction to those who stoned their friend. But in time, they accepted the sincerity of Paul's conversion.

His calling to preach the Gospel to the gentiles came about through his knowledge of their Hellenistic leanings and the pantheistic society thriving under Roman domination. He traveled throughout Asia Minor, Greece, Rome and the Mediterranean, as an itinerant preacher.

For his efforts, he suffered every kind of deprivation, starvation, illness, imprisonment, stoning, and mob violence. He was misunderstood, even by other Christians—especially the Judaizers, who wanted to convert gentiles to Jewish law as well as to Christ. Along with these hardships, his eyesight was failing. Eventually he was executed for his faith in Rome.

"If Christ be not risen," Paul wrote the Corinthians, "then is our preaching vain, and your faith is also vain...If in this life only we [Christians] have hope in Christ, we are of all men most miserable." [I Corinthians 15:14, 19].

How foolish and hopeless, in other words, to put one's trust in Jesus, **unless** Jesus did, *indeed,* rise from the dead, and

His resurrection promise is a reality.

A man with all the privileges, intelligence, and opportunities that Paul had does not throw away every natural advantage, just so he can chase after a leaf in the wind. From that fateful encounter with our Lord on the Damascus Road, Paul **knew** he had encountered the risen, conquering Lord of hosts, the One in whom he could place his full confidence and his future. As he later wrote, *"I am persuaded that neither death, nor life, nor angels, nor principalities, nor powers, nor things present, nor things to come, nor height, nor depth, nor any other creature, shall be able to separate us from the love of God, which is in Christ Jesus our Lord."* [Romans 8:38-39].

Those two verses were written out of *experience*, not from the closet of a reclusive philosopher! Here was a man who had put his faith to the test. **He knew!** And he acted, based on that knowledge and confidence. As a result, the history of Europe and the known world was forever changed.

If this book accomplishes anything, I hope it encourages you to make a personal investigation into the claims of Christ upon your life. The spiritual gains from a day-by-day walk with God will amaze and bless you beyond all imagination.

POWER TO CHOOSE. If we truly had it within our own ability to carve out a perfect little niche for ourselves, you can be sure we would never choose heartache and pain and suffering. Those would definitely be scratched from the list of life's options. *Forget pain*, you say. *Forget financial worries. Forget broken relationships. Forget sickness and death; let's eliminate that altogether from our journey. The people I love should live forever.* We would scratch anything unpleasant from the list. Given a free rein, we would choose only great vacations to places like Cancun or—what?—Tahiti? Sunsets and fabulous days at the beach. Fishing in a mountain stream with that special grandkid who shares your love for fly casting.

Or maybe skiing in the Alps is your "thing. Take your pick.

Fantasize about what would make you and the people closest to you the happiest. Maybe it's lazing around in a hammock, watching butterflies flutter across the lawn. Or reading a book to a child and sharing a laugh.

Maybe your list would include a bigger house, a newer car. Money in the bank. And since you've left out all the so-called negative experiences in life, you may or may not want to include a college fund for the kids. But learning does enhance one's enjoyment of life, so why not? Of course, death has been eliminated, so life insurance policies won't be part of the Big Picture, but dabbling on the stock market sounds fun.

Sure, you say, *why not?*

Only one thing is wrong with this daydream.

It isn't life!

And we aren't God.

Thank God, we're not God! Can you imagine the mess we'd be in, if we were in charge? But I leave that subject to another book—providing *you* write it!

No, this book is about our *POWER TO CHOOSE.* **Our power to choose is directly dependent upon our choosing *Him!***

If we are Christians, we already know that **He has chosen us in Christ Jesus**. That happened way back there in the Garden. When sin entered the world, God already had a plan, the perfect plan for our salvation. All we have to do is accept His plan and His gift of salvation. There isn't a thing we can do to deserve it. We can't earn it. We can't manipulate or justify or finagle our way into the Kingdom of God.

We must simply choose God. Simply acknowledge our need, our lostness, our alienation from Him and from one another.

Have you ever had a child place a broken doll or toy in your hand? If you have, you know how we must appear in

God's sight. All any of us needs to say is, "Fix me, God. I'm broken inside. The mainspring is bent, and I'm a mess. Unless you put me back together and mend me from the inside out, I will always walk crooked and keep falling down and never get it right."

If you haven't come to that point in life's journey, I hope you will choose God's will over your own right now. It will save you a great deal of pain and misery, if you do.

Step Number One: Choose God.

This is the initial phase, when you choose to get right with God. You ask Him to reset your priorities, give you a whole new life, clean you up from top to bottom.

This He gladly does. You and I basically stand there, like a kid getting a scrub-down from Mom or Dad on Saturday night. You bask in His glorious love, a little amazed maybe, while His searchlight beams such light and power and joy into you that you *know* you've been born again.

Step Number Two: Choose God.

This is the phase where you get a slight jolt or wake-up call from God. You've been going along fine, taking in the Word of God and enjoying fellowship with other Christians. Life has been going along pretty well, or maybe your experience with Christ is still a little uncertain—like surfing at Waikiki. You ride a few pretty good crests, get a little cocky, and then—*slam-dunk!* You're in the drink. Or you hit the beach—uh, prematurely—get dragged in the undertow with your mug scooping up sand halfway to China. Well, maybe not that far, but you get the idea. We tend to get pretty banged up by life before we truly see the folly of self-effort and rely on God to see us safely along life's perilous path.

So, you start to realize, *Maybe I'm not as advanced in my Christian walk as I thought.* You start assessing your use of time and the friends you hang with. You wonder where you will be in another five years, and if God doesn't want your life to count for more. So far, you're right on track. God *does* have a plan for your life. Only it's going to take a whole lot more than graduate school, or donating a few hours on weekends to find out just what He has in mind. You haven't a clue. But *He* knows. So you **choose God**—again. And again—and *again*.

Step Number Three (or maybe it's Step Number Twenty; it depends on God, and it depends on how briskly you're walking.) Anyway, **Choose God.** And don't stop. Don't ever stop.

By now the habit of choosing God has become fairly well integrated into your faith-walk. Most of the time, you may not feel as if you're doing anything very special. But what you're doing is developing spiritual muscle. After all, it took more than one can of spinach before Popeye got those arms! Probably he felt like he'd gag on spinach sometimes, but he kept popping those tin can lids and pouring in the green veggies. But you never heard him complain when Bluto showed up, dragging Olive Oil by the scruff of her scrawny neck, did you? That's because Popeye was prepared—in advance of need.

Now I grant you, not all of life's catastrophes and trials are willing to wait until we're super-human Christians. In fact, I don't think God ever intended it that way. Paul reminds us that "we have this treasure [God's Spirit of power] in earthen vessels" *--why?--* "so that the excellency of the power may be of God, and not of us." [II Corinthians 4:7]

So that's what's going on, you may respond. Exactly, my friend. God richly endows us with His blessings. He loads us down with blessings! He gives us His Spirit and His power. He gives us His love. He sends people into our lives to bless us. He gives us natural attributes that are often truly amazing. Not all of us will be athletes, or architects, but we will *all* receive our share of personal gifts. He is a generous God, because He is rich. He created the universe. He owns it all! There isn't one iota of stinginess in His nature. He gives *good* gifts. "Every good and perfect gift is from above and comes down from the Father of lights." [James 1:17]

But there *is* one thing He does *not* allow us to usurp or take from Him: His majesty and His glory. Remember that. He is God. We are finite, His creation. That is why we make a big mistake if we attempt to "evaluate" or "appraise God's actions critically" [Romans 2:1]. (Job knew this, too.)

Opposing God in a critical spirit is dangerous business. It should not to be confused with God's willing invitation to honest inquiry. A critical spirit leads to the hardening of one's heart, while the other approach denotes teachability. In Jesus' parable of the Sowing of the Seed, this is brought out quite clearly. God doesn't say, "Don't think." Rather, He commands, "Learn of me."

So whether it's Step Number Seven or Seven Hundred and Forty-nine, **choose God.** Any other choice leads to destruction.

The Call to Obedience.

Count on it: Somewhere along the Journey, we are likely to encounter what I have come to regard as The Christian's Walk through Fire. It entails cleansing, a purifying of the spirit that is dependent upon only two things: God's Power, which is never in short supply [we have His Word of promise on that], and...our obedience.

Now what do I mean by obedience?

Are we talking robots? No, not at all. Obedience is not simply our recognition of God's Sovereignty and the fact that the events of our life--indeed, our very life!--are in His hands. That He is Who He claims to be. That He is faithful. That He is trustworthy and just. That He is love. And power. And strength. And everything else we could ever possibly need.

In other words, *He* **is our Life!**

We can stand in His strength alone.

Our getting through the next minute, or the next hour, or the next ordeal does not depend upon anyone else but God. **He is sufficient.** *We are complete in Him.* [Col. 2:10]

World without end. Amen. In fact, even if the world as we know it *should* end, He "abides faithful." [II Timothy 2:13] He cannot be otherwise. He is God. Drum that fact into your head. Stake your life on it: *He will not fail you!*

"MADE PERFECT IN WEAKNESS" [II Corinthians 12:9] Having walked through the fire, we marvel, just like Shadrach, Meshach and Abednego, that we have come through intact. How is this possible? *Only* because the Son of God has taken the heat for us and brought us through a refiner's fire that produces pure gold in our lives!

So dispel any foolish notions about how you're going to reprogram your life and avoid the pitfalls and the pain. I guarantee you will not succeed, no matter how hard you attempt to sail through life on a fair breeze. It simply doesn't happen that way in an imperfect world.

Hopefully you'll never face The Big Trauma that so many whose stories appear in this book have gone through. But you *will* encounter your share of trouble. It comes with the territory. If you're breathing, you cannot escape God's Plan for Planet Earth.

Our walk is one of discovery, the daily unfolding of an exciting tapestry of intricate designs and colors. At times, you will shake your head, thinking your life is nothing but a tangle of threads and ugly burlap. But every once in a while God will give you a peek at the other side, where all the warmth and beauty of living reflects God's pleasure at your sometimes clumsy but mostly faithful tapestry weaving. The pattern will be unique, a fitting testimony to the life you and God are working out together.

Daily you have the **power to choose.** And as you take up your cross daily and follow Him, you discover the secret to

joyous living: **Power is supplied as we choose Him.**
PUT NO CONFIDENCE IN THE FLESH.

Even though Lazarus was raised, he had to undergo physical death again.

Members of the New Age movement focus on out-of-body and near-death experiences. This fascination with the paranormal and attempts to put things into some kind of scientific context has serious drawbacks. They are not rooted in the reality. The end result is that many people today tend to dismiss vital issues related to their timespan on earth. Some reject the existence of heaven and hell and judgment and contend that Christians are using scare tactics.

It is easier for them to accept fanciful, unsubstantiated "tunnels of flashing lights" and other emotionally based ideas than to face the truth, that even those who claim to have returned from "beyond" are still going to experience physical death. The part about judgment makes them uncomfortable, so the New Ager prefers to adopt a "wait and see" attitude: "Life is now, right? As long as I'm sincere, everything will turn out okay." What pathetic posturing!

Hey, guys and gals, let's get serious!

Life is too precious to waste it on fairytales.

I'll take my chances with the Great God of the Universe. He's been around forever. Longer, actually.

But I digress! It concerns me greatly that Eastern religions and their derivatives seek to minimize the impact of death through the postponement of judgment. The avoidance of pain is another damaging component of this thinking. It is unrealistic—the antithesis of Christian thinking, which is not afraid to examine life under a microscope and tell it like it is.

Only Christians can honestly look death in the face and not quake. They are the *only* ones with an adequate answer to the question of what happens after death.

The delusion of "No Fear" proponents is that somehow

they can delay or avoid giving an accounting for their actions. They seem to forget that death is a very real part of life, just as birth is.

Our brief lifespan is over faster than the wink of God's eye. *Then what?* It's a valid question. Philosophers have wrestled with the meaning of our existence, the meaning of life and death, and the existence of a Supreme Being from time immemorial. Their best ideas fall pitifully short of God's personal revelation of His eternal plan.

Jesus said, ***"I am the resurrection and the life. He who believes in Me, though he were dead, yet shall he live. And whosoever liveth and believeth in Me shall never die. Believest thou this?"*** [John 11:25-26] Jesus' statement cannot be dismissed out of hand. He had just raised Lazarus from the dead! A man who had lain four days dead in grave clothes; a stinking corpse—not a pretty sight. Talk about bold living! Our Lord is anything but faint-hearted.

But even when we are reeling and weak with shock, worn down and weak with despair, His boldness and His life can raise us to newness of life. **Count on Jesus.** He faced reality and life's most heartbreaking issues unafraid!

Jesus didn't walk around wearing a "No Fear" T-shirt. He was too busy releasing His fellow travelers from the bondage of fear and superstition, and the desperation of their human condition. Hallelujah, what a Savior!

Jesus didn't deny the human condition. He didn't whitewash or *prettify* life. He didn't sentimentalize. He saw life for what it is, and He transformed human clay into glory!

He forgave a prostitute and taught her to hold her head up again without shame. He rescued a leper from social ostracism. He made the blind to see and the lame to walk. He loved a tax collecting scoundrel and turned his greed to generosity. He rather appropriately—from the Jews' perspective—cast a tormented man's demons into a herd of swine!

He made it possible for people to love themselves, *as is.*

He empowered. He loved. He died. He rose again. What more convincing proof do we need of His awesome power and majesty and love?

"For it pleased the Father, that in him [Christ] should all fullness dwell; and having made peace through the blood of His cross, by Him to reconcile all things unto Himself." [Colossians 1:19-20]

"Forasmuch then as the children are partakers of flesh and blood, He [Christ] also took part of the same; that through death He might destroy him who had the power of death... and deliver them who through fear of death were all their lifetime subject to bondage ... Wherefore in all things it behooved Him to be made like unto His brethren, that He might...make reconciliation for the sins of the people. For in that He himself hath suffered being tested, He is able to succor those who are also tested." [Hebrews 2:14-15, 17-18]

GOOD NEWS OF OUR DELIVERANCE

The Good News is that Jesus Christ takes us *beyond* the grave. He delivers us from our shallowness, our desperation and our sin. The resurrection of Christ promises us a new body. Christianity is the only religion that doesn't avoid judgment, the consequences of sin, and moral issues, but deals with them by delivering us, transforming us, and making us new.

The world's religions try to appeal to people by fabricating plausible lies. Only the Gospel faces life squarely and shows us the way out of our dilemma. Our deliverance is found in Christ alone.

So, glorify God in your bodies, but put no confidence in the flesh.

Chapter 9. Incentives To Help Us Overcome

By now, it should be evident that God gave us the power to choose in the Garden, and He has been wooing His creation ever since, to decide. *Will we go our way, or His?* Our allegiance is the issue at stake. Depending on our answer, many of the other choices that influence and effect our lives are set in motion, either limiting and cutting us off from, or opening up to us, a whole range of possibilities.

Hopefully the examples given in this book will help you see some of your own vulnerabilities and how to sidestep some of the pitfalls that impair our ability to make healthy decisions and deal effectively with the challenges that cross our path. What matters, and what governs our success or failure, is how we choose to act or react in the midst of crisis and pain.

Inescapably this brings us back to the Sovereignty of God. Ultimate wisdom demands and requires us, as thinking men or women, to align our wills with His. This is central to the prayer our Lord taught the disciples: "Thy will be done, on earth, as it is in heaven." [Matthew 6:10; Luke 11:2]

Let's examine what happens when we consciously choose to walk in the Spirit instead of the flesh, when we yield *in faith* and thus agree to let God work in and through us, instead of struggling through it in our own strength.

1. We are no longer alone. I daresay we were never alone, even before we realized that fact, but the certainty of it often takes a tremendous burden off our shoulders. Jesus our Burden Bearer took upon Himself the cross and bore all our sins, that we might be pardoned and set free.

When we align our wills with His, we no longer have to wrestle with the old ways of the flesh [First Order thinking and solutions]. We walk in His strength, in His power.

When His will becomes ours, we become inseparably bound together; my pain becomes His pain; my joy becomes His. This holy compact, or the sharing of His will, involves traveling the same road. It means that God brings us under the umbrella of His protection, entrusting to us the integrity of His Name and trusting us to act accordingly. In return, we trust Him to act and to deliver, in accordance with His Word.

The prophet Amos recognized this need to align ourselves with God's will, when he wrote, "Can two walk together, except they be agreed?" [Amos 3:3]

Left to our own resources, our sense of aloneness and our need to find relief often prompt us to take desperate measures. Resorting to the ways of the flesh [First Order thinking and solutions] causes life to degenerate into a soap opera or oldtime serial flick, as we gallop from one cliffhanger to the next.

Agreement with God removes the alienation and adversarial relationships that are so common to the human experience. God's act of reconciliation replaces our powerless posturing and isolation with peace and certainty.

2. We discover we have a capacity to deal with life that far exceeds our own limited resources. We are no longer solely dependent upon our own cleverness, our own talents, our own "spiritual bankroll," to cope with life. As the stories throughout this book portray—particularly in Sections Two and Four—God's generosity and the outpouring of His Spirit in the midst of life's trials are truly astounding. The outcome is *not* up to us. All He asks is our trust. He takes care of the rest. *"God will supply all your need according to His riches in glory, by Christ Jesus."* [Philippians 4:19]

3. We find ourselves free of turmoil. When the primary issue of trust is settled, it's like entering the eye of the storm at sea. Having been at sea many times in my twenties, I know what it is like to be on a ship, surrounded by a tremendous wall of raging wind and water and noise, and yet experience perfect calm. In Christ, we have peace in the midst of the worst of life's storms. We have *"the peace of God, which passes all understanding."* [Philippians 4:7]

4. We have Light and Vision to deal with whatever is on the darkest road ahead of us. *"I will make darkness light before them, and crooked things straight."* [Isaiah 42:16] What an assurance when life seems like a collapsing tunnel and the light at the end grows dimmer with every step!

One such couple is Rick and Marge, who landed in Las Vegas with a fair amount of savings and big dreams of setting up a new franchise. At first, their new restaurant was a big success. Customers liked their low prices and friendly service. They were keeping their heads above water, and based on projections for the coming year, Rick and Marge would reach the break-even point in approximately eighteen months. Things were going so well that they planned to expand, using the initial capital investment money they recovered.

Seven months later, Rick slipped coming out of a freezer and landed on his back. He took two aspirins and expected everything would be fine in the morning.

The next morning he couldn't get out of bed. Marge called the paramedics, who rushed him to the emergency room. There he was told he was suffering from back spasms. He was loaded down with prescriptions for pain and muscle relaxants and sent home.

Leaving one of their teenage sons to keep an eye on Dad, Marge went off to the restaurant. In her absence, one of the help had made off with last night's till. She went to the bank and replaced it, made sure the other employees had things under control, and called home to see how Rick was doing.

During her absence, Rick had rolled in his sleep and somehow the pain was even more excruciating. In the background, while talking to her son on the phone, she could hear Rick's agonized scream. In a panic, she left their most responsible employee in charge and drove her husband to another hospital By now, she was sure Rick must have broken his back, and the first hospital should have caught it, when they x-rayed him.

Again, they spent an interminable amount of time waiting to be seen, and again, they were told it was merely back strain. They were given more pain medicine and sent home.

Over the next several days, their lives grew more chaotic. Rick was almost out of his mind with pain. Finally, having made the rounds of several doctors' offices, they wound up back where they started at the first emergency room.

Marge insisted the emergency room doctor take another look. Exasperated, he ordered additional tests, since the initial x-rays had turned up nothing significant, other than the swelling of tissues around the spinal column. What he discovered was that Rick was in the advanced stages of spinal cancer.

Rick was admitted and treatment to save his life began in earnest. Within three months, they had gone through their entire life savings. They had to sell their business to pay for chemotherapy and radiation. Their daughter in college had to drop out, and their home went into foreclosure.

Rick had gone through several surgeries, and while the prognosis was still uncertain and he was now permanently confined to a wheelchair, Rick and Marge seem curiously unaffected by this terrible turn of events.

Their secret? They know God has His hand on them.

In the midst of their financial reverses, God led them to a fellowship of caring Christians, who continue to stand with them in their fight. They would never have chosen to undergo what has happened to them, but the spiritual dividends have been tremendous. They have never known such peace, such spiritual power, or such *love*! And with their faith intact, they know that even death cannot take away the love God has put in their hearts—for each other and their children, and for their brothers and sisters in Christ, who are helping them get through each new day.

5. We lose our fear of temporal things. Through our faith, fear loses its grip and its power over us. We have God's promise that He will "in no wise cast out" [John 6:37] or forsake us. [Isaiah 42:16]

The child within our trinitarian make-up fears abandonment above all. The fear of abandonment and power-lessness, of not being able to control our outward circum-stances, underlies our deepest fears. When we realize the *impossibility* of our ever being alone, because God is "a very *present* help in time of trouble" [Psalm 46:1], we can relax. This not only optimizes our chances for clear thinking, it also allows us to experience God's "perfect love [which] casts out fear" [I John 4:18] and promotes healing.

Living without fear also empowers us to go on living.

6. We have hope, which empowers us to move forward. Just as fear floods and shorts out our engine, hope is the gasoline that fuels our faith.

A year before, Curt had lost his wife to cancer, after twenty-four years of marriage.

Reflecting recently on how blessed he had been in his first marriage, Curt admits that all had not gone smoothly since his second marriage. The reason has nothing to do with his decision to remarry or the lady in question. It seems that his sons by his first wife couldn't accept his decision to remarry.

Yet when my friend met Betty, they both immediately recognized God's gracious leading. Soon their paths became one at the altar.

What happened next must have been extremely heart-breaking, as both his sons turned their backs on him. (Older parents who have encountered similar censure and attempts at emotional blackmail will understand immediately how hard it was for Curt.)

Only Curt's mature faith saw him through this family split. Fortunately, his wife Betty, an extraordinarily loving woman who had had her share of trials in her first marriage, is no stranger to heartache and sorrow. Together they stood firmly by their commitment to each other.

Their courage and long experience with the Lord got them through a great deal last year—although I doubt even the pounding their house took in Southern California's earthquake compares to the trials of the spirit they both have endured!

Hope makes us unafraid, so that we view the future as having unlimited possibilities.

7. We are free to love more effectively. If we have lost sight of what it is to love, our relationship with Christ can help us face our mistakes. Although it is never wise to take love for granted, in many cases (but not all), I have seen clients recover that which "the locust has devoured." [Joel 1:4]

Five years ago, Rory thought his life was over. In his pursuit of material gain and success, he had neglected his family and violated the marriage vows he had exchanged with his high school sweetheart. His wife Molly had every reason to leave him, but, surprisingly, she hadn't.

Instead of being grateful, Rory continued to run around till all hours, and frequently heaped verbal abuse on his family whenever he made a "pitstop" at home. Like a house of collapsing cards, his life continued to deteriorate. As his business began to fail, Rory ignored the warning signs of a marital break-up, while he fought to resolve problems caused by his own lack of attention to detail and a crooked business partner. He borrowed money and took on more jobs than he could handle with his present crew, in a last ditch effort to keep his business afloat. Driving himself day and night, he finally collapsed with a bleeding ulcer, then had complications during surgery that nearly cost him his life.

"God really had to drop the sky on me, in order to get my attention," Rory recalls. The end result was that when he finally had no physical strength, no financial resources, and had run out of excuses, he called on the Lord.

Although he had "accepted Jesus" as a youngster, God had played no significant role in his adult life. Now, suddenly, he was faced with the very real possibility that he might die.

He was a failure as a husband and father. He had lost credibility and solvency as a building contractor. He had run up an enormous pile of debts, which his wife would have to pay off, if he died—his hospital bills already amounted to more than he'd earned in the past ten years!

"I realized then that I had nowhere else to turn" Rory explains. "Like the Prodigal Son, I finally came to the point where I stopped kidding myself. I had to hit rock bottom, before I was willing to swallow my pride and ask for God's help. I guess you could say that was the day the old Rory died, so that the Lord could take this sick and dying man and replace all the rottenness with His new life inside."

The inner changes were dramatic, but. Rory's physical recovery was more gradual. He tends to believe it was God's way of keeping him from getting "a big head." Still not out of the woods, he summoned Molly and his children to his bedside and asked their forgiveness for his lack of love

"God gave me a new appreciation for my wife and kids," he relates. "I can't express how much it meant to have Molly sticking by me during the next few months, while I sorted out the mess I'd made of my life and got my priorities straight. My respect and love for Molly grow stronger every day. We're still struggling to recuperate financially, but I've got my family back, and I've got the love of my Savior to see me through.

"No man can lose everything and come back from the grave without knowing a miracle has taken place. No one knows better than me how many blessings I've received."

8. We Gain Confidence. Our walk in the Spirit with our Companion on the road instills within us a sense of **certainty** as to the outcome of our journey. We come to understand that "He gives power to the faint, and to them that have no might, he increaseth strength." [Isaiah 40:29] Each step taken in faith brings us a new appreciation of Jesus' statement, *"All power is given unto Me, in heaven and in earth."* [Matthew 28:18]

9. We Receive Comfort. As we have fellowship with Christ in His sufferings, the Holy Spirit enables us to find meaning and solace in His presence. We find strength and comfort in His Word, as we learn that we are not the first, nor will we be the last, to experience suffering and trials. We also find encouragement from the fact that Job emerged from the crucible of suffering with his strength renewed. He "prospered and [was] blessed" [Job 42:12-17], more than before.

10. We Experience Power. God's grace carries us through, empowering us to make decisions and to act with wisdom and love. We don't need to second guess God. He wrote the book of your life; He knows how it's going to turn out. Trust Him! *"Be strong in the Lord, in the power of His might."* [Ephesians 6:10]

Chapter 10. We Have God's Assurance.

Exodus records how God called His people forth, leading them in perfect safety through great danger and adversity. In I Corinthians 10:1:1, Paul reminds us that the Israelites passed safely through the Sea, because they were careful to remain under the moving cloud—visible as a pillar of fire by night—which signified God's presence and power in their midst. The Egyptians perished. The *only* difference between these two groups was Whom they chose to trust and follow.

Just as Joseph learned in Egypt, after long years of wrongful imprisonment and spiteful mistreatment, and just as the Israelites learned after forty years of wandering in the wilderness of their unbelief, we can have confidence that:

1. God is a good and loving Father.

2. God will not let any experience touch our lives that He cannot use it for our betterment and ultimate blessing.

3. God did not cause our misfortune or suffering, any more than He brought on Job's many catastrophes.

4. God is the Source of all blessing.

5. He never abandons us, and when all else has been said and done, He is still our life, our hope, and our salvation.

That is why we need to set our minds and hearts upon seeking God's will, especially in times of severe trial and heartache. We rarely have a choice about what happens, but we *do* have a choice about how we face it. We need to ask ourselves: Will we place ourselves in the way of blessing, or allow ourselves to become bitter? Will we spoil the memory of those who are precious to us by allowing the bitterness of sin to creep in and rob us of our peace?

Job's Wife: One Way of Facing Heartache.

I believe we should view Job's wife with a degree of human compassion. After all, she had lost as much materially and emotionally as her husband. Those were her children, too. And while she might have been spared the boils and other physical ailments that afflicted Job, her soul must have been sorely vexed by having to watch his flesh rot off his bones, day after day. Job's wife suffered greatly.

She was stripped of everything but her health; her position as a wealthy man's wife was gone. And then she had to sit there and watch her husband slowly shrivel and die before her very eyes. She had to put up with the incessant drone of philosophical debate under her roof—what was left of it!—and probably grew tired of extending hospitality to Job's friends at all hours of the day and night. It could not have been easy for this dear lady, and on the surface, she seems entitled to an occasional lapse of faith.

Here she is, helpless to change the circumstances of her life, sorrowing over her dead children, and watching a man who once was strong and virile—"a tiger" in her eyes—now wither and become even more helpless than she. Her words reflect large portions of anger, grief, sadness and self-pity.

"Curse God and die." Why did she say that? Have we never been tempted to say the same thing? Have we never felt a guilty relief when a loved one who has suffered greatly is finally dead and beyond pain?

Is it not human nature to rationalize that suffering is a *bad* thing, and, therefore, death is merciful, maybe even desirable?

This outlook is nothing new. It emanates from the flesh, from our finite understanding of pain, suffering and what is unexplainable. It also reveals how distorted our thinking is regarding the nature of God. Job's wife infers that since her husband's faith has been misplaced, he might as well cock up his toes and die.

Job's wife's remark refutes everything that experience had taught her husband Job, especially about the sovereignty of God. Where was Mrs. Job during the good times? How had she failed to notice God's hand in their prosperity? In the faces of her children as they came into the world?

Yet this is so like what happens to most of us when life is going along smoothly. We grow complacent and smug about "our" accomplishments. Ironically, we forget the part God has played in our lives—although we are quick to blame Him for anything that goes wrong!

At this point, even knowing Mrs. Job's distraught condition, we have to part company with her. Like Eve, she has been taking counsel with Satan. Fortunately, Job doesn't swallow the bait, as did Adam. He knows the "Author and Finisher of his faith" [Hebrews 12:2] and, no matter how bad his situation gets, he will not deny his faith or depart from His presence, either physically or spiritually.

We also need to recognize where Mrs. Job's line of reasoning takes us, if we press it to its logical conclusion. Her words go right along with those who support the world's view of suffering, abortion, euthanasia, and the handling of such "inconveniences" as pain and disabilities, temporary and permanent, which set some people apart from their more fortunate brothers and sisters.

Do not such questions, so often couched in compassionate language, seek to legitimize the Jack Kervorkians of this world? The Hitlers and the Nazi death camps? The purges of Stalin and Mao Tse-Tung and Idi Amin?

The rationale behind many heinous acts perpetrated against countless thousands, even millions, of the human race is never far from any of us. We need to guard our hearts against going along with "easy" solutions. The way of the cross *is* difficult, but the end result of choosing God's better way brings incalculable spiritual dividends.

Can we afford to judge God? I think not.

As "sincerely" as Job's wife may have meant her advice, our task is neither to justify suffering, nor to second guess God. Our job is to trust Him and believe in His goodness. Ultimately, that was Job's answer to his wife and his friends: ***"Though He slay me, yet will I praise Him."*** [Job 13:15] Strong language, but then, Job was dealing with those whose spiritual eyes were dimmed by sorrow and whose spiritual hearing aids were turned inward, instead of being tuned in to the Lord and His sovereign will.

Job is an extraordinary man, bold even in moments of the most extreme anguish. His response should give us hope when we've reached the end of our tether and we can't endure any more heartbreak.

Like Job, we, too, can praise the Lord of hosts, choosing not to let anything rob us of the victory and the love and the richness of life God intends us to have.

If the person you love has been taken from you, *regardless* of the circumstances, bless God for the time you were able to share. Refuse to fall prey to the tempter's snare!

It's not our job to analyze God's role in our grief, but rather to align ourselves with His perfect sovereign will. Not that we could fathom the mind of God anyway. Far better that we focus on Who God is, exploring His nature and appreciating the fact that He has the situation under control.

That doesn't mean we have to *like* what has happened. We are not expected to spout syrupy platitudes. All we need to do is be honest. For God understands, better than we ourselves will ever comprehend.

Heartache Over the Senseless Death of A Loved One.

Pastoring a growing church halfway between the coast and Salem, Oregon, Jim and Nancy were putting up their Christmas ornaments for the holidays a few years ago. A group of high school church kids, including their own daughter

Cheryl, stopped by for hot chocolate after making the rounds caroling various shut-ins.

Suddenly one of the young people suggested playing a practical joke on the new youth minister. "Let's toilet paper his house," someone suggested impulsively.

Jim and Nancy tried to discourage the idea, pointing out that it was nearly eleven o'clock. "Don't forget, Sunday School at nine," they cautioned.

But there was no dissuading the lively group. Something of a practical joker himself, Jim saw no harm in their having a bit of innocent fun. Promising to return within the hour, the revelers departed, armed with several rolls of toilet paper, while Jim and Nancy shook their heads fondly over the irrepressible hijinks of their young people.

Forty minutes later, the phone rang. A drunk with a 2.3 blood alcohol level had driven his car through a stop sign only four blocks from their home. Both cars were totaled. Cheryl, in the front passenger seat, was dead on arrival at the hospital. Fortunately, nobody else, including the drunk driver, suffered more than minor lacerations and contusions.

The drunk woke up in jail. Jim and Nancy never fully recovered from the loss of their only child, even though they continued to serve the Lord in that quiet community faithfully. Where once Cheryl's joy and laughter had brightened their lives, there would always be a void in their hearts..

Eight years later, Jim died at that same intersection, when a logging truck with bad brakes slammed into the driver's side of his car. Nancy now commutes to her job in Salem on weekdays and continues to teach Sunday school to the high school age group. All her daughter's classmates are grown up now, married with children of their own.

The other kids in their daughter's youth group, though visibly shaken, went on with their lives. A few dropped out of Sunday school. It was hard watching their pastor and his wife grieve. They missed Cheryl, too, and hated being reminded what a narrow escape the rest of them had had that night. They couldn't understand why God would let their friend die in such a senseless accident.

Others questioned why a wholesome A and B student, who had never done a mean, spiteful thing in her life, should be lying in a grave, while a drunk with two previous DUI arrests got off with a $1,000 fine and another suspended license, which meant nothing to him anyway, or he would never have been driving the night he killed their friend Cheryl.

Where was the justice in that?

These seem like valid questions and concerns. But the question that really needs to be asked is, What impact did this incident have on the survivors? On the parents? On Cheryl's classmates? On the drunk driver? Did any of what happened that fateful night make a difference? Or was the world essentially the same—no better and no worse than it was before the car crash?

These are the questions that thousands of grieving parents and families ask themselves each year. The slaughter of innocent bystanders on our highways, in our neighborhoods, and in our communities is epidemic.

So please, God, what does it all mean?

As far as I can determine, there *are* no pat answers. There is no single answer that will satisfy the heart cry of those left behind when senseless tragedy strikes.

We don't have a cookie-cutter God who gives "canned" answers. What we *do* have is a God of compassion and infinite wisdom. He alone can wipe away our tears and mend our brokenness. And in the process, we discover we are no longer the same.

We may *appear* the same, but like Shadrach, Meshach and Abednego walking in the midst of the fire, we discover we have not gone through it alone. God our Father weeps with us and holds us dear to His heart, for He, too, lost a Son because of the sinful and thoughtless acts of a lost humanity. He mourns with us, yet His love transcends His grief, allowing His forgiveness to transform the guilty and reconcile us to a "better resurrection" [Hebrews 11:35]. When we encounter this One who is "like unto the son of God" [Daniel 3:25], we also find the power to get through what is impossible in our own strength to endure or comprehend.

So, did Cheryl die for nothing? Did her parents mourn in vain? Did their faith supply certainty only for eternity, when they will be reunited with their daughter? Or is there a message we can glean from their experience for the here and now?

I do not ask this facetiously, but because God's Word confirms to my pastor's heart that **there is no valid way we can separate what happens to us down here on earth from the life to come, when we shall behold Him face to face and share fully in His resurrection power.**

If not one sparrow falls to the ground without God's notice, can we not also conclude that what happens to each of us matters to God? I think we *can* have that assurance.

Not all of us will receive our answer or see lives transformed because of the sacrifices we make here on earth. But rest assured, the best rewards and the greatest solace are reserved for those who wait upon the Lord.

The Heartache of Mental Illness.

A dear childhood friend of mine knows the truth of this all too well. During his daughter's late teens, she suddenly began to experience schizophrenia. Over the years, her illness became so severe that it became impossible for him and his wife to leave her unattended. This kept the parents from enjoying much of a social life, taking trips together, or pursuing many of the career opportunities their friends had.

Both Christians, these grieving parents decided not to institutionalize the daughter, even though it would have freed them of a tremendous responsibility. The path they chose is not for everyone, but they were convinced that to abandon her went contrary to their faith. They chose to be inconvenienced, in order to demonstrate Christ's love to her.

Caring for those with on-going needs demands sacrifice. Those involved in the care of loved ones who are handicapped, disabled or terminally ill tend to feel isolated. Because their responsibilities often keep them homebound, they are prone to being misunderstood and even criticized for not attending church more often, or participating in other types of activities less encumbered people have time for. They need a double portion of God's grace and our understanding and love. I am often amazed by these selfless people's cheerful acceptance not only of the one in their midst who is suffering, but also of others who carry similar burdens. Nobody makes a better friend than the person who has also walked in your shoes.

The Heartache of Betrayal.

Selfishness often manifests itself in amazing ways. I was once called in as an expert witness in a court case where a wealthy social climber had forged her elderly mother's signature and removed a large sum of money from the woman's bank account. When the bank discovered the forgery and threatened prosecution, it wasn't long before the entire family became embroiled in a court hearing to determine the mother's mental status and competency. A power struggle soon developed to see who would control the aging mother's financial affairs.

The daughter presented herself in court as an extremely cultured, well dressed woman. She and her husband lived in one of the wealthiest sections of Atlanta, where her work as a dedicated civic leader had advanced her husband's career in stocks and investments. She drove a new car, shopped only the most expensive stores, and belonged to the local country club. Obviously the daughter did not *need* her mother's money;

but she sure coveted it.

Why would anyone want to take money from a simple farmer's wife, who had sacrificed to put her daughter through one of the most prestigious private colleges in the South? The only motive I could come up with that held water was the daughter's deep-seated resentment against her mother—that, and social ambition.

One complaint that surfaced during the trial was how much the daughter hated having to wear homemade, though quite presentable clothing all through college. This may seem a small inconsequential detail to many, perhaps, but to the daughter, her mother's pinch-penny economics felt like the ultimate humiliation.

After college the mother continued to scrimp and save so that her daughter could go on to graduate school. Shortly thereafter, the daughter married well, had four lovely children, and somewhere in her climb up the social ladder, her mother became an unsuspecting accomplice in the grand scheme all dream makers fabricate for themselves.

Ambition [fueled by the need for love and acceptance] soon blossomed, and the mother basked in her daughter's growing popularity. While her daughter and her son-in-law worked, she went over to her daughter's beautiful house each day. She cleaned, cooked, did yard work and cared for the children after school. She received no compensation and in many respects, was treated more like a maid than a parent.

When her daughter, with the help of the court system, finally gained full control of her mother's life savings and committed her to a nursing home, the shock proved too great. The mother went into shock, unable to accept this ultimate betrayal by the very person she had spent a lifetime trying to help. Eventually, the older woman's retreat from reality became permanent. Unlike most people put in nursing homes, this elderly woman had an iron constitution, even though it was generally conceded that her mind "snapped." Ironically, the last time I heard, she had spent the past ten years babbling such dysphemisms as, "They stole my money!" and "Dirty rotten crooks."

Outbursts of this sort must be a source of perpetual embarrassment to her daughter. "Vengeance is mine; I shall repay." [Romans 12:19] I can't help thinking that even when we are supposedly "not all there," we may be serving God's purpose!

If you're ever tempted to believe in a "hell on earth," a trip to some of our fashionable retirement centers may prove illuminating. Certainly it will make you think twice about committing the sin of idolatry by misplacing your affections. Give God first place by laying up "treasure in heaven, where neither moth nor rust corrupt, and where thieves do not break through and steal" [Matthew 6:20] For "where your treasure is, there will your heart be also." [Matthew 6:21; Luke 12:34]

Our Response Arises Out of Where We Place Our Trust. When life leaves us chopped down to our knees, when our hearts fail, and we're in shock and disbelief, our loving Savior opens His arms and gathers us to His heart. He is a Man of sorrows and acquainted with grief. Who better to comfort and sustain us in our hour of need?

When there are no words to express our inmost feelings, He knows. He walked this earth, experienced all the temptations, all the uncertainties and challenges of daily living, all the harshest truths of human spitefulness and sin. He knows what it is to be reviled and spat upon. He knows what it's like to have a friend who no longer believes in you, who can't understand what you're going through and wants no part of your experience or your pain. Jesus knows. He has seen it all, been touched by every infirmity and problem common to the human experience.

He who knew no sin became sin in our stead. He walked

those dusty, swarming streets to Golgotha, his back scourged and lacerated and filthy. Sweat and blood mingled with His tears for a lost and dying world. Blurring his physical sight, but never His vision. Jesus knew our salvation could come no other way than through His paying the ultimate cost and enduring the pain by dying in our place. His ears, deafened by the rabble scorn, were attuned to the great eternal King of the Universe, as He dragged that heavy executioner's cross.

It is only as we enter into Christ's sufferings on this deeper level that we begin to glimpse the grandeur of God's plan for our lives. Even then, we catch only a faint glimpse, compared with the awesome scope of the Father's love.

We must also remember that "He endured the cross" because of the knowledge of what lay beyond that fearful, twisting, black vortex called death—not extinction and oblivion from pain, as some would urge us to settle for, but the glorious Resurrection Power that was demonstrated that first Easter morning at the Garden tomb, and later when Jesus appeared to over five hundred of His followers.

Resurrection! Not a trifling bit of emotionalism upon which to pin our hopes. No! We have a God Who cares. A God who acts on our behalf, who is *active* in His concern, and never more so than when we are most vulnerable and needy.

Today God still calls His children out of bondage, whether self-inflicted or the result of others' actions. His mercy impels Him to seek us out and raise us from the pits of affliction, sorrow and despair. He is our Good Shepherd, our Savior, our Friend who "loves at all times." [Proverbs 17:17]

Coming Up: Section Four demonstrates how exercising the power to choose liberates us to deal with difficult and heart-rending circumstances—not unlike those faced by thousands of families today.

I have asked Mrs. Patterson to go into considerably more detail, in order that you can see the dynamics of faith and love at work even in the midst of her family's pain.

Of course, every person's situation is uniquely their own. Because God expects us to **think** and **respond under His leadership**, no one should attempt to use this or any of the other stories in this book as a road map or model for dealing with his or her own situation.

All the authors of this book join in recommending to you the limitless resources in Christ, which inspired that great Baptist missionary, William Carey (1761-1834), to write:

"*Believe* great things of God.

"*Attempt* great things for God.

"*Expect* great things from God!"

In other words, Be Bold, Be Believing, and Be Prepared for A Great Blessing!

Section Four. POWER TO CHOOSE

SCOTT

**The Story of One Family's Heartache,
As Their Son Became Involved in
Drugs and Crime,
and
What Happened When They Chose to Love,
Regardless of the Personal Cost and the Pain**

by

Sandra Patterson

Author's Note

What I have set down in the following pages actually happened. Names, locations, and some details have been changed in order to preserve the anonymity of those involved. I apologize to anyone reading this who would have preferred a shortened account. However, it seemed to me the only way to provide sufficient and convincing proof that we do indeed serve a Great God of miracles. That is my *only* reason for going into such detail about Scott's troubled teen years and our family's struggles—that and a desire to show the desperation of our lives and the longsuffering and gracious work of God in our midst.

Admittedly, there were times when Scott's life had become so reprehensible as to be completely abhorrent to us that we had to battle our own human tendency to turn our backs and run for cover. The pain was that intense.

For those into denial, this may prove a difficult read; you may not be ready for this. It's okay to skip this section, if you'd rather.

For those who may be experiencing similar trials, I want you to know that "*nothing is impossible with God*" [Luke 18:27].

One of the ways we overcame our self-loathing and the temptation to reject him was to harken back to an earlier time when we *could* love Scott, freely and without reservation. I admit that meant going back a long way! But by fixing our thoughts on memories of the loving child he once was, we managed to work through the anguish and fear that we had somehow produced a monster that even God couldn't love, or that our faith in God might not be enough.

Today, I am happy to testify that God is the *only* One in whom you can place your full faith and trust and know He will not let you down. *He will not fail you.* Being human, Glenn and I made many mistakes as parents. But through it all, God was *always* faithful. He alone deserves the credit for the miracle He brought about in all of us, as He moved to break down the barriers and, very literally, saved Scott's life.

Chapter 1. Our Wake-Up Call.

The phone rang at five minutes to midnight. Both my husband Glenn and I were sound asleep. It took a few seconds for Glenn to respond.

He stumbled to the phone across the room and picked up the receiver, "Hullo?" he mumbled sleepily,

"What? Arrested!...Where? You mean—" Glenn paused, letting the impact of the caller's statement sink in. Suddenly I was fully awake, every nerve screaming. Just my husband's muffled responses to the caller convinced me that our son Scott had really done it this time.

Glenn asked a few more questions, then replaced the receiver. Shoulders sagging, he came over and sat down on his side of our bed. His voice was expressionless with shock when he spoke. "That was Stan Baker's wife calling. He and his brother are in jail in Boise. There are warrants out for Scott's arrest. For Interstate flight."

In agonized, choked tones, he described to me as much of the situation as he knew: Scott evidently had become involved in some burglaries. Stan and Don Baker, the two men who had invited our son to help them build a cabin in the woods, had been arrested with stolen goods. Facing up to sixty-five years in prison if convicted, the two brothers had named our son as playing a key role in the burglaries. In fact, as part of the plea bargaining process, they had "fingered" our eighteen-year-old son as the "brain" behind the crimes!

A feeling of impending disaster had hovered over my spirit for the past week and a half. Now I understood why. My first glimpse of Stan Baker, who had helped restored our son's dilapidated old 1957 Chevy truck, had sent a shiver of cold fear through me. I had only seen him twice before our son, always restless, had announced he was going up to Idaho to help this man and his brother build a cabin, trading his labor for having his engine rebuilt. I had pleaded with Scott to stay, but my words had fallen on deaf ears.

As a Christian minister, my husband had invited an evangelist friend to stay with us that coming week during a series of meetings in several churches in the Phoenix area. We had been hoping Scott would be around to hear him and counsel with him. Instead, our son had timed his departure only hours before our evangelist friend arrived.

Scott left early on a Wednesday morning. Instantly an inexplicable, unshakable sense of foreboding welled up within me. I found myself praying frequently for him during the next few days. He didn't call when he reached his destination; my heart felt weighed down like lead with fear.

Meanwhile Glenn and I were busy with people in our home for group Bible studies. We accompanied our friend as he presented the claims of Christ in fourteen different churches in the area. A great many first time decisions were made. It was a wonderful week, over too quickly.

The following Monday, as I sat at my desk in the office where I was employed as an insurance claims adjuster, I received a collect call from Scott from Boise. Some strain in his voice made me ask, "Is everything all right, Scott? Have you been 'good'?"

A typical mother's question, but there was more to it than a mother's natural concern. Though I admit we had tried to be sensitive to the pressures to conform placed on all three of our children as "preacher's kids," we had had more than our share of problems over the past seven years with Scott, our oldest. Oh, he understood my question, all right, and why I asked it.

His answer was terse, a put-off. "Yeah, sure, Mom. I'll be home Saturday." He hung up, and I immediately began to pray. I knew something was wrong. But I never dreamed what he had become involved in until that telephone call at midnight the following Friday.

Chapter 2. Only A Matter of Time

Glenn and I tossed and turned, weeping and praying aloud, for the rest of the night. That midnight phone call had robbed us of any false hopes that our teenage son might at last be getting his life together. Only a month before, Scott had successfully completed two years' probation for possession of marijuana. We were frightened for Scott, for we couldn't understand why, with all his advantages and a Christian upbringing, he could just turn his back on our family values and become involved in burglary. We didn't have any details, but it was devastating enough, just knowing he was in serious trouble.

The next morning Glenn and I went through the motions of putting breakfast on the table for our other two children, Shelley, a year older than Scott, and Chris, who was three years younger than Scott. They may have noticed our lack of animation and enthusiasm, as we went through the formality of a prayer at the table, but Shelley and Chris were too busy sharing the funny papers and news of last night's college football scores to comment. Perhaps they thought we were tired from the demands of pastoring a growing church. Anyway, we weren't quite sure what to tell them, so we said nothing.

Saturday mornings always were busy with laundry, house cleaning, yard chores, washing cars, and picking up the week's accumulation of casually discarded items around the house. Glenn had to put the finishing touches on his sermon for Sunday, so he gave me a peck on the cheek and quietly let himself out. I was glad he had something to take his mind off our heartache. I was so used to handling housework routinely that nothing really could take my mind off Scott. I felt almost as though he had died. In fact, I was almost tempted to think he'd probably be better off dead. The idea of my son spending time in jail, perhaps most of his life, was crushing emotionally.

After I finished up the main housework, with only two interruptions from church members who were looking for Glenn, I took refuge in my room and had a good cry. I wondered if I hadn't thrown the last eighteen years of my life out the window. Had all my efforts to share Christ and instill His values in my son been a waste? I felt as though Satan was really sneering at me. Although I felt like conceding that perhaps Scott just hadn't caught on, the thought of Satan enjoying my misery made me angry.

"Lord! Surely this can't be happening! Please show me what you want to accomplish through all of this. Scott has been headed in the wrong direction for years. Please show me what to do," I cried, pounding my fist into the pillow. "And please help me experience your forgiveness and victory, even in this. Either that, or...or let me *die!*"

Even after I finished pouring out my heart to the Lord for help, I still felt the Accuser's presence. *Where was God?* I thought in a flash of weakness. Why hasn't He kept Scott out of trouble? How could we have gone so wrong? How had we failed Scott? I found no comfort or help in that session with the Lord. But having unburdened my heart, I felt more peaceful. I drowsed briefly, until Scott drove up with a friend. He slammed the front door, noisily dropped a suitcase of dirty laundry and his athletic gear in the middle of the living room, and cursed when he didn't immediately spot someone to wait on him.

"Hey, Mom! Where the hell are you?" he said in a rough tone.

I was tempted not to respond from my bedroom. I supposed his dictatorial manner was intended to impress his friend. However, I did want to talk to him, so I rose reluctantly. Pushing a lock of hair off my forehead and biting my lip, I breathed a prayer for God's help and opened the door.

"Scott, hi. What's going on?" My eyes went from my son to his swarthy friend, whose hair looked none too clean. I didn't like his looks, but I tried to look beneath the surface when dealing with Scott's companions. "Hi. Dave, isn't it?"

"Yeah." Dave never talked much. He never looked me in the eye either. His head was down, his hair falling in his face.

"Mom, I'm starved. When's lunch?" Scott sprawled in an easy chair, one leg swinging over the arm.

"Chris has already started a fire in the barbecue out back. I expect we'll be eating soon," I managed, surprised at how calm and even my voice sounded.

"Goofing off, huh? Where's Dad?" He glanced around casually and winked at his friend Dave.

"He's at church, you know that. Listen, you don't have to wait around. If you want, I'll make you some sandwiches." My voice caught nervously. "Scott, we need to talk."

Scott looked sharply in my direction, perhaps expecting me to scold him for making a wreck of the living room right after I'd cleaned it.

"What I have to talk to you about is important, Scott. And private," I added, looking straight at him.

He shrugged and rose to his feet. "Be just a sec, Dave. Gotta humor Mom here," he commented, following me into the master bedroom.

I closed the door and came right to the point. "Scott, your father got a phone call last night from Stan Baker's wife. The Baker brothers are in jail in Boise. She says there is a warrant out for your arrest."

"You're kidding," he said, standing with his weight on one leg, his shoulders crooked. Then he turned on a wide-eyed smile and reached out to nudge my arm. "Hey, Mom, if those guys got into trouble, that's their problem. Me, I ain't done nothin' wrong."

Scott knew how much sloppy speech irked me. Right

now, I didn't care. "Scott, you've got to turn yourself in! I'm scared for you," I whispered hoarsely.

Scott's expression told me he was busy "spacing" me. He shrugged. "You and Dad have too wild an imagination. I told you, everything's cool."

I took a step toward him. "Listen, Scott, don't lie to me. I know something is terribly wrong. Your only hope is to turn yourself in."

"Later, Mom," he said, already turning the doorknob. "Stop comin' off the wall all the time. I didn't rob anybody."

"I never said you did, Scott! But you know more than you're telling me," I said, standing my ground.

"You're hallucinating, Mom. See ya!" He left the room before I could open my mouth to reply.

I followed him out to the kitchen where he was rummaging around for the makings of a few sandwiches. He dragged out some soft drinks and a quart of milk. "Dave, pour us some milk, my man."

"There's ham in the refrigerator, Scott, behind the lettuce and bacon," I volunteered, leaning dejectedly against the wall.

"Hey, Mom," he shot me a casual glance, "you're getting out of shape. Maybe you should join a spa or work out with my weights." He laughed, and Dave ducked his head with a guffaw. "Yes, sir, look at all that *ham-m-m*!" he said, slapping together four "big ones," as he liked to call his Dagwood style sandwiches. As a finishing touch, he topped off the lettuce and tomato with saltine crackers and another slice of bread.

"Hope you enjoy your snack," I said and wheeled around before he could see the tears.

Heartsick, I went out to see how Chris was coming along with the barbecue. Chris was turning the baked potatoes and corn-on-the-cob, wrapped in foil, on the grill. He was our youngest, quiet and the total opposite of his noisy brother. He seemed so poised at fifteen.

"Hi, honey," I said, coming over to inspect his work. "About ready for the meat?"

"Give it five minutes," he suggested. "I've got a friend coming over to eat with us around one-thirty."

"Fine. Looks like you've got everything under control out here." I gave his arm a squeeze and looked back at the house, my eyes misting over.

Chris always caught everything. "Hey, Mom, don't take it so hard. Scott's got a few rough edges. He'll be okay."

I wiped my eyes with the corner of my apron. I didn't want to unload my burden on Chris. I was just grateful he wasn't following in Scott's footsteps.

"Hey, I got two A's and three B's on my report card. Wanna see?" Chris whipped out his school record to distract me. 'How's that for improvement over last spring?"

I took the card in my hands. The letters swam in a blur of tears as I peered at it. "I—uh—forgot my glasses, Chris, but you're right. You've really picked up those grades in English and history. Good work."

Just then Scott leaned out the sliding glass door. "Mom, Dave and I are going to take off now. See you later."

"Okay," I said. "Try to get back before dark."

His only response was the sound of his truck revving up on the front drive. In a minute, the noise was gone, and I was left with only questions...questions. Clearly, it was just a matter of time before our world came tumbling down around us. In the meantime, we had to go on living somehow, despite this mounting pain deep inside.

Chapter 3. The Waiting Is Over.

The next few days were relatively quiet. Glen and I were almost able to dismiss that phone call as a bad nightmare.

Almost. Scott was busy with his friends and kept late hours as usual. He wasn't home much, but that was nothing new lately. He seemed defensive, even when we tried to engage him in casual conversation. So we waited, we prayed, and we hoped.

The following Wednesday, about three in the afternoon, I received a frantic phone call at the insurance office where I worked. It was Chris.

"Mom! Scott was just arrested by the F.B.I. I can't stand it, Mom. It was so terrible."

My heart fell like a cold stone in my chest. "Chris, are you all right, honey?"

His voice was full of anguish. "I was just pulling up in front of the house with the other kids in my car pool. Scott came out of the house with a couple of guys—Don and Bernie, I think. Anyway, Scott was just opening the door of his truck when this tall guy in a big Lincoln Continental drove up real fast from down the block. He jumped out with a gun the size of a cannon in his hand and said, 'F.B.I. Freeze, or you're dead meat.' Oh, God, Mom. I was so scared."

"Yes, I know, Chris. What happened next?"

"Well, two more cars drove up fast. They had Scott spreadeagle against his truck while they frisked him. Then they put handcuffs on him and put him in one of the cars. What's going on, Mom?"

I swallowed hard. My throat was so dry it was hard to talk. "I'm not sure, Chris. I think he's involved in something pretty serious, but I don't know quite what. Listen, I'll be right home. Meanwhile, call your father and let him know what's happened."

Chris started sobbing. "I already tried the church, Mom. Dad must be out calling, or something."

"Just try to remain calm. Chris. I'm so sorry this has happened. I'll be home as soon as I can." I hung up. Listening to Chris's heartbroken sobs was more than I could bear. I sat for a moment with my head in my hands.

Annie, who worked at the next desk, looked over at me. "Sandy, are you okay?"

"Something's come up. I...I don't feel very well suddenly." I dabbed at my eyes, but the tears just ran down unchecked.

"Why don't you go on home? I'll let Mr. Forbes know you're not feeling well," Annie suggested.

"Thanks, Annie, I think I will...go...home." I stood up, grabbing my handbag, and picked up my jacket. "I'll probably be in the morning. But if I'm not here first thing in the morning, just tell Mr. Forbes I'm sick, will you?"

"Sure thing. Hope you get to feeling better."

"Me, too." I felt numb as I pushed open the door and walked out to my car. I sat dully behind the wheel, keys in hand, for several minutes before I could compose myself enough to start the car. I dreaded what might confront me when I got home.

Chris was waiting for me, his face tense and pale. We embraced in the living room silently.

"Mom, Dad called to say he's been held up at the hospital. Mrs. Wacker is in bad shape, and he promised to stay with the family until the doctor came. He said he'd be going directly from there to evening Bible study. He said he was sorry, but I was to tell you he wouldn't have time to check into what happened with Scott until tomorrow."

My hands clenched involuntarily. At a time like this especially, I wished my husband had an ordinary job, so he could drop everything and just concentrate on his own family's needs, instead of always being on call. I knew he had no choice as a minister, but right now *I* needed him. Wasn't I a church member, too? My sense of rebellion was fleeting, but for a moment I felt as if the most important person in my life had abandoned me. Obviously, I was on my own.

"Chris, let's fix a quick bite of supper," I suggested. "We

need to keep Scott in prayer. There's a lot of confusion right now, but we mustn't lose hope." I started toward the kitchen, wondering how much Chris actually knew. It seemed as though most of our family crises led me straight to the kitchen and food lately. I started rummaging in the cupboard out of habit, hardly aware what I was pulling down from the shelves.

"I'm not hungry, Mom." Chris trailed behind me and stood by the counter, fingering the formica, his eyes down. "This afternoon was like Scott died, Mom. It's like he's thrown away his whole life."

"Let's not think defeat, honey," I said, wielding a can opener. "I guess it *was* pretty humiliating for you, having all this happen in front of your classmates."

"I don't care about that so much. Right now, I can only think about Scott and what this is going to do to his life." I saw a tear form on his lashes and hang there.

"Tell you what, Chris. After dinner—" I was just going to suggest we track Scott down when the telephone rang. We both raced for it.

It was Scott. His voice was subdued, almost inaudible. In the background, I could hear the noise of voices and metal clanging. Everything sounded as if it were echoing.

"Hey, Mom. I guess Chris told you what happened this afternoon."

"Scott! Where are you?" I exclaimed, relieved to hear his voice.

"They've booked me into the Glendale jail." His voice trailed off.

"What did they arrest you for?" I asked.

"Interstate flight. They're supposed to arraign me in the morning and then transfer me to another facility. This is the only night you can see me before I get moved." He hesitated. "Mom, could you come?"

"Of course," I said without thinking. "What are visiting

hours?" I felt so strange, as though I were planning to visit a hospital or something. This was my first trip to a real jail.

He cleared his throat. "Listen, I gotta go now. Can't tie up the phone. You can see me any time before eight o'clock tonight." He hung up.

There was so much I wanted to ask him. So much I wished had never happened. *Where had we gone wrong? Why had Scott become so rebellious and angry in recent years? Why could we never seem to reach him?* No answers came. I wanted to beat on the wall and scream out my frustration to God. I wanted to, but I didn't.

"What's up, Mom?" Chris asked, watching me with solemn eyes.

"I'm going to see Scott after we grab some supper. Want to come along?"

Chris shook his head. I can't say I blamed him.

Chris and I opened a can of soup and made peanut butter sandwiches. We sat at the table, sipping our soup in mugs and trying to get down the sticky peanut butter. The sandwiches tasted like cardboard as we tried to swallow them down. We might as well not have tried. Our thoughts and emotional level were never lower, as I tried to visualize what Chris had been witness to that afternoon.

"Boy, they sure were tough, those G-men," he said, shaking his head and blowing into his soup. "They wore these mirror sunglasses and looked about ten feet tall. The one holding the gun on Scott wore cowboy boots." He shuddered at the memory.

"How awful it must have been for you," I said, feeling resentment toward Scott for putting his brother through an emotional wringer. "What did the kids in your car pool say?"

"Not too much right then. But one of the parents phoned later, before you got home. They're pulling their kid out of the car pool."

I smiled grimly. "I guess they don't want to associate with criminals. Well, don't take it too hard, Chris. I have the feeling someone dropping out of the car pool is nothing compared with what your father and I are going to encounter. This is sure to cause a negative reaction from some of our church members."

"Do you think Dad will lose his job?"

Chris's eyes searched my face anxiously.

"We'll just have to put that in the Lord's hands, too, won't we? If we don't have enough understanding Christians in the congregation who will stand with us and pray us through this crisis, we'll be better off somewhere else anyway." I hadn't had much time to speculate on how Scott's actions might effect his father's ministry. "I'm sure your father will share his situation with some of the leadership tonight," I added.

Chris shrugged. "I sorta like it around here. I have a lot of friends. But if it means leaving—well, okay."

I reached over and patted his hand. "Chris, you're really great. Don't ever think we take you for granted. I thank the Lord every day for your good sense."

"I'd never ever put you and Dad through all the hell that Scott has. I've seen the way it's hurt you both." Chris ducked his head.

I felt the tears, not far from the surface. How could I have had two such different sons? I dearly loved them both—Shelley, too—but Scott was so impulsive, restless and willful, while Chris showed a maturity and understanding far beyond his years. How I thanked God for Chris's emotional support and kind words at that moment!

"Hey, Mom, do I have to finish this sandwich? Chris asked, changing the subject.

"No, of course not. I can't choke all of mine down either. Just not hungry, I guess."

I rose and started moving plates to the sink.

"I feel kinda wiped out. Guess I'll just finish my homework and get to bed early." Chris sounded emotionally drained. "I hope there's never another day like today."

"Me either. Well, I'd better hurry, if I'm going to see Scott before visiting hours are over."

Just then the telephone rang. Glenn was on the other end of the line. "Sandy, I'm sorry I can't be there with you and Chris. Lousy timing."

"That's all right, Glenn. I'm going over now to see Scott. Maybe I can find out what's really going on and what he's being charged with," I said, brushing my hair back, a nervous gesture. Catching a glimpse of myself in the mirror across the room, I realized my eyes were like burned out sockets of grief. I made a mental note to dab on a little make-up to disguise my ghostly pallor.

"I'm going to let the folks know how much Scott needs prayer right now. Better that they hear it from me than from another source," Glenn said.

"What sort of reaction do you think the church people will have?" I asked. I could picture headlines screaming out all sorts of sordid things in the morning papers.

"Probably better not say much until we have a better idea what he's been charged with. This whole thing may have been blown way out of proportion. I'll just tell them what we know, which isn't much."

How I admired Glenn's steadiness in a crisis. I felt anything but calm. "I guess it's best to take it one step at a time," I agreed. "Anything you want me to tell Scott when I see him tonight?"

"Just that we're praying for him, and hope he will turn his life completely over to the Lord." His voice broke, revealing his concern. "Well, gotta go, Sandy girl. Keep your chin up."

As I replaced the receiver, Chris was standing in the doorway. "Mom, it's six o'clock. You'd better hurry."

I moved a little more deliberately than usual, fighting to organize my thoughts and actions despite the shock I felt. "Could you feed the dogs while I'm gone? I'll be back as soon as I possibly can."

"Sure, Mom. Be glad to. Say 'hi' to Scott for me." The stricken look on his face, as he stood framed in the doorway, remained in my mind for days. There was no escaping the fact that Scott's actions had left a profound mark on the entire family.

I pulled the front door shut behind me. Getting into the car, I drew a deep breath, braced myself, and turned the key in the ignition. I felt as though I was moving deeper into a maze, one fraught with uncertainty and danger that would alter our family's history forever. Would life ever return to normal for us again?

Chapter 4. The Slammer

The Glendale jail looked so foreboding as I walked across the parking lot and entered the building. This was the first time I had ever been to a jail. It felt strange, being stopped by security downstairs.

When I stated the purpose of my visit, the deputy asked for my social security number. She turned to a computer and typed my name and number onto the screen. I showed no "priors;" in fact, I had never even gotten a traffic ticket. The woman gave me a strange look and told me what floor of the jail to proceed to.

Installed in a cement encased shaft, the elevator reverberated the smallest sound. Its heavy doors boomed loudly as they opened on the floor where Scott was incarcerated.

Stepping out, I walked through a series of thick metal doors, accompanied by ominous clicks and clangs. I could easily see why jails are referred to as "the slammer." Due to jail construction, they are very noisy, harsh places.

After I waited a few minutes, Scott was ushered in on the other side of a thick glass window. Dressed in ill-fitting blue dungarees, he already looked different: His hair was untidy, and his eyes were wide, almost unblinking. He tried not to show any emotion, as he slid into the seat opposite me.

"Scott, what's going on?" I asked.

Carefully cautious and noncommittal, he shrugged. "Not really too sure. Well, I guess I have an idea, but it's hard to see why the police think I'm involved."

"You're holding back on me, Scott." I surprised myself how calm and logical I sounded.

"Hey, the Bakers did something wrong. But that doesn't mean I had anything to do with it. That's all I meant."

"Well, what do you want us to do for you? How long are you going to be in here?" I was busy studying his face and body language.

He shifted in his seat. "I'm to be arraigned in the morning and then transferred to Phoenix to await extradition. Thanks for coming to see me, Mom," he added.

"We still love you, Scott. We don't know what's going to happen, but we want you to know that we love you. Your father was sorry he couldn't come tonight. He has Bible study."

Scott made a wry face. "That's nothing new. I didn't really think he'd find time—"

"Scott!" I blurted out in ready defense of his father. "Your father cares very much about you. It just so happens this is Wednesday."

"Yeah, sure, Mom. Anyway, I'm glad *you* could come. Do you think you could get hold of a lawyer? Maybe he could get me out on bail after they transfer me tomorrow." He glanced around, as though he expected to catch the custodial staff in the act of eavesdropping.

"I could contact Mr. Irving, who helped us when you were arrested a couple of years ago," I offered.

"That sounds cool. Sure. Ask him." Scott seemed at a loss for words. Usually he had plenty to say.

"I'll get in touch with him in the morning," I promised. "When is the arraignment? I want to be there."

"Nine, I think." He licked his lips nervously. "If they don't have anything on me, they have to dismiss charges after forty-eight hours."

"What *are* the charges, Scott?" I asked, hoping he would open up.

"Interstate flight to avoid prosecution." His eyes went wide with feigned innocence. It was obvious he wasn't going to reveal anything, probably fearing it would implicate us or work against him.

"We'll be there in court, honey," I told him. "Our prayers are with you."

"I believe in Jesus, Mom," Scott said, his eyes down for the first time. "No matter what comes down, I'm not afraid."

How I wished I could touch my son at that moment! If only I could offer some solace or encouragement. But that thick glass, the constant clang of doors closing, elevator traffic and footsteps up and down the hall added to the cold, unfriendly atmosphere. "Dad said to tell you: You need to turn your life over to the Lord, Scott. If you had already, none of this would be happening."

"Don't preach to me, Mom. You mean well, but this isn't the time, okay?" He looked embarrassed and resentful at being reminded of his failure to live up to what he knew was right.

"I don't mean to sound critical, Scott. We're just concerned. But I feel so *helpless!* What can I do to help?" I felt a sense of futility rising within me.

Scott shrugged silently.

"Is there anyone you'd like me to contact for you?" I persisted. "Other than the attorney?"

"No, I already got hold of Linda." Linda was his girl friend, a quiet girl who no more fit into his wildness than we, his family, did. "She and her brother are coming to see me as soon as I get transferred out of here."

He looked so young sitting there, I nearly lost my composure altogether. "Scott, Linda seems like a really nice girl, but some of your friends are—well, they're unwholesome, to put it mildly." I felt myself becoming "hooked" into discussing a topic I knew I should avoid.

"Lay off my friends." Scott's face darkened with anger. "You and Dad come off the wall too much. Mellow out."

"Oops, sorry," I murmured. "You're right. This discussion isn't doing either of us any good right now." I swallowed hard. I prayed silently that the Lord would help me keep the door of communication open.

Suddenly Scott became solicitous of my wellbeing, something totally out of character for him. "Listen, Mom, I think you'd better be getting home. I don't like you being out late. It'll be dark soon."

"Thanks for the concern about my safety, Scott. I think you should be more concerned about your own future. I just wish--" I stopped myself before I started dumping on him. "We'll just hope and pray that some mistake has been made."

"There's no way they can prove I had anything to do with what the Bakers did, Mom. Play it cool," he advised with a wink. "I'll be all right." Somehow his voice lacked conviction.

"Scott, frankly I'm having a hard time handling the idea that my own son is behind bars..." I blinked back the tears.

"Steady, Mom. I'll probably be out of here in the morning. Like I said, they haven't got any proof." He stood up, terminating the conversation.

"See you in the morning," I responded dully. I backed

away from the window, not wanting to lose sight of him as he left the cubicle.

"Later." I could see his lips form the words. He raised his hand briefly, then spun on his heel and walked out.

Slowly I picked up my purse and jacket. He was trying too hard to act unconcerned, as though nothing were wrong. *Perhaps he's afraid to share his real feelings, for fear someone might overhear*, I thought.

As I made my way back to the elevator and waited, I tried to analyze what was really going on in his mind. If only he had turned himself in! Perhaps then things would have been different. Perhaps he was only shielding someone else? Whatever his involvement, he had rejected our advice to surrender to the authorities a few days ago. Now he would have to face the consequences of his actions.

I wondered how we, his family, should react. Should we detach ourselves completely and assume a "hands off" policy? Should we isolate him from our family circle and let him face the music alone? And if we did, how would this affect the chances of his making a 180° turn around to the Lord? I tried to put myself in his shoes.

Forget what others think, I told myself. *What matters is what becomes of Scott. We can't be soft on him, but at the same time, we need to continue to show him our love. And the unfailing love of Christ, Who came to save sinners like us and Scott.*

If we cut ourselves off from Scott when he was hurting and confused, who would he turn to? The answer was obvious: He would become part of the "system" behind bars. His counsel wouldn't come from the Lord, but from men much harder and more experienced in crime than Scott. I could easily see the danger of Scott becoming lost altogether to our family, to society, and to God.

Even as I contemplated putting our family's reputation and

Glenn's future ministry on the line for Scott, I recognized that Glenn and I also had two other children, both deserving of consideration. They could easily face ostracism from friends and classmates. Chris had already been rejected by the family that pulled out of our car pool. That wouldn't seem like anything, compared with what might occur, once Scott's arrest and trial came to light.

But I mustn't let panic push me to the brink of despair, I reminded myself. Maybe Scott was telling the truth. Maybe he wasn't involved in anything serious enough to send him to prison. I resolved just to live each day as it came, remembering always to express my gratitude to the Lord for those things I could genuinely praise Him for.

I couldn't honestly thank Him for where Scott was, or what he might face tomorrow in court. But I could praise Him for happier days with Scott, for His giving me strength and peace, despite this aching pain deep within my heart. I could thank God for my two other children and pray for their Christian faith not to waver in the midst of this. I could thank Him for Glenn, for his solid, unshakable faith and for his love.

I resolved not to waste time wishing things were different. I would thank Him for circumstances that seemed hopeless. Even if it took prison, it would be worth it, if Scott surrendered his life to God. I already knew He had His hand on Scott, who at a very young age had placed his faith in the Lord Jesus Christ as his Savior. Even though Scott was now rebelling against the sovereignty of God, the love relationship was still there. After all, the Lord had promised never to leave nor forsake His children! As J. Hudson Taylor had discovered well over a century before, "Even if I am unbelieving, He abideth faithful." God's faithfulness was not conditional or reliant upon Scott's success or failure. *God is Who He is*, regardless of what we His creation might do. What a tremendous God we have, so trustworthy, so praiseworthy!

There in the jail parking lot, I raised my eyes to scan the heavens. For the first time in weeks, I experienced the peace I so desperately needed, and I turned Scott *entirely* over to his Lord, for Him to deal with as He chose.

Chapter 5. The Plot Thickens.

Glenn and I were at the U.S. Marshal's office promptly at eight the next morning. We wondered what the office clerk must be thinking, as we introduced ourselves as Scott's parents, especially when she told us what he was "guilty" of doing!

"Four counts of burglary; transporting deadly weapons across two state lines, interstate transportation of stolen property, and interstate flight to avoid prosecution, just to mention a few," the woman said, nonchalantly leafing through the thick file on her desk.

We looked at her in a daze. The impact of the clerk's words almost knocked the breath out of us both.

""What?! That's just not possible! Scott hasn't any weapons or guns in his possession since he got back from Idaho. Why, we've *never* had a gun in our home," Glenn tried to explain.

"He probably didn't bring anything to your house, because it might implicate you," she said. "At any rate, the APB bulletin says he was armed and should be considered extremely dangerous."

"Well, he's in custody now,"I interrupted. "Can you tell us when the arraignment is scheduled? I understand he's to be transferred to another facility later today."

"The arraignment took place last night in judge's chambers," she said, checking her files. "Your son is probably already in custody in the Phoenix jail."

Glenn exploded. "Without the benefit of an attorney?"

"We assigned a public defender to represent him last night."

"Well, is there anywhere we can post bail?" Glenn asked.

"Bail is set at $100,000. That's what the Federal Judge specified," she said, looking at us over her bifocals.

"One hundred thousand! We can't possibly come up with that, Glenn," I whispered, beginning to feel frightened. Scott had certainly landed himself in over his head this time.

"If I might make a suggestion," the woman said, softening a little. "I'd wait until the Federal Marshal's office hands him over to the County as custodian until the State of Idaho can extradite him. It's very possible the County may not require such high bail."

"When will the County set bail?"

"He's being handed over this morning, so it shouldn't take more than a day or so." She closed the file and placed it in the "out" basket with a stack of forty others.

"Thank you very much," I mumbled, my heart heavy with resignation.

Glenn and I headed for the elevators. Getting back in our Chevy station wagon, we drove to the Phoenix jail, where County prisoners were housed.

When we reached the front desk, a policeman promptly referred us to the detective assigned to Scott's case.

Detective Schneider sat us down in a small office and shared what he understood of the situation. "I can only tell you that your son faces up to sixty-five years in prison, if convicted on all counts. He transported guns—a large quantity of handguns, rifles and shotguns—across the borders of two states, along with stolen property. You're lucky he wasn't shot on sight. The print-out describes him as 'armed and extremely dangerous.'"

"I can't believe you're talking about our son, Scott," I

said. "There must be some mistake."

"No mistake, ma'am. He and two other men broke into the homes of several prominent citizens in the Boise area. They took jewelry, money, guns, antiques and a lot more, all worth many thousands of dollars." The police detective, like the Marshal's clerk, assumed Scott's guilt. Because of our system of justice, I had always assumed the police department also would not *assume* guilt without a fair trial. Was I ever wrong!

"When he arrived home, none of those items were in his truck. I can vouch for that," Glenn asserted.

"He probably stashed it somewhere with a 'fence,'" the veteran police officer said, bored and a little amused by our naivety.

"He couldn't be involved!" I persisted. "When he returned home, he was completely broke. He had to borrow money from his brother to put gas in his truck."

"When he hit Pioche, he stole gas from a gas station," the detective continued as if he hadn't heard me. "He was stopped ten miles out of town and returned to Pioche. He paid ten dollars for the gas, and the charges were dropped. Lucky son-of-a-gun is all I can say," he said, shaking his head.

"What?" Glenn exclaimed. "You mean he was stopped for stealing gas, and the arresting officer didn't spot all those guns and stolen goods you say were in his truck?"

He smiled. "Seems strange, I'll admit. But the officer probably didn't connect the APB out on an armed robber with a kid stealing gas. In these small western towns, it's a wonder they didn't blow him away."

Glenn let out a long breath. I could see the muscles in his face tighten. "Okay," he said, "let's look at this logically: If the police stopped him and returned him to Pioche, surely they would have checked to see if there were any other warrants out on him."

The detective shrugged. "So they slipped up. Happens all the time. Funny thing, the police can make a mistake. But the criminal can't make even one. Anyway, your son is facing extradition now."

I decided to seek this man's advice. "Detective Schneider, what would you recommend regarding extradition?"

"Personally, I would advise him to waive extradition. That way the State of Idaho would have to pick him up in forty-eight hours and issue specific warrants. All we're holding him on right now is an F.B.I. warrant for Interstate flight."

"It would only be a matter of forty-eight hours more in jail before the State of Idaho would come get him?" Glenn asked.

"Give or take."

"I see. When will he be given an opportunity to waive extradition?" I asked. This cat-and-mouse game was starting to give me a thumping headache.

"Tomorrow morning at nine o'clock."

"We'll see him in the meantime and advise him to waive extradition," I said.

Glenn rose first and shook the man's hand. "Thanks for taking time to speak with us. I still think they have the wrong person, though. Scott has been in trouble as a teenager, but never for anything connected with violence and firearms."

"We know our son, Officer," I added with a nod. "He's definitely not the type of person who would steal guns."

"I can only go by the facts given me, ma'am," Schneider repeated. "He's one dangerous *hombre*, if you ask me."

"Thanks for your time," Glenn said wearily. "And thanks for the advice."

Our hearts sank even lower. What we'd heard made our minds reel. How could Scott have possibly become involved in anything of this magnitude?

Because visiting hours weren't until later, we returned

home to pray. Our two other children were out, Shelley in class at the community college and Chris at his high school. We were grateful for the solitude, as we went to our knees in the living room beside the couch and wept. All our dreams for this handsome son seemed to have vanished. What would become of him? Although never a good student, Scott had always been bright and promising. His outgoing personality and charm had always attracted others.

But then again, Scott had had scrapes with the law since age twelve. Most of his friends, like him, were underachievers with chips on their shoulders. Plenty of family scenes had occurred over his drinking, smoking pot and breaking curfew—all to no avail. Scott had deliberately turned away from us and our family values. Somehow in all his rebellion and anger, something we never could understand, he had fallen into even worse company than we'd realized.

Despite our heartbreak, we came up off our knees determined to continue to show him the love of Christ, just as we had in the past. We decided that God's love was "tough love," but it was also tenacious, "unwilling that any should perish." [II Peter 3:9]

We were helpless to give Scott any help in his dilemma, except to love him. He must face the consequences for his actions, whatever they might have been. But we pledged ourselves before the Lord to stand by him, regardless of what it did to our reputation in the eyes of other Christians and our neighbors. Even if we should lose everything—job, home, savings—nothing mattered, if we could prove to Scott that he was loved—by us *and* by the Lord.

Glenn returned to his church study after lunch. He had a hard time getting his mind on Sunday's message, but we were in full agreement that he couldn't neglect his flock.

As soon as they came home from school, I explained to Shelley and Chris that Scott was in even deeper trouble that we'd thought. They took the news pretty well, though Chris seemed more deeply affected.

"He really blew it, Mom. He's done some rotten things before, but there was always hope before that he'd straighten himself out." Chris broke down and wept.

Shelley shared her brother's concern, but her reaction seemed more egocentric. "Mom, if this gets around, it's going to ruin my popularity on campus."

I was shocked. "Shelley, dear! How can you say that? Can't you see Scott's whole life is on the line here? Don't you even care?"

"Sure, Mom. But I have myself to think about, too. My friends will never understand." She teased a strand of hair over her ear and patted it down, as she stood in front of the big mirror over the couch.

I saw Chris wince. "Some sis you are! I've had a lot more beefs with Scott, but I would never take an attitude like yours," he accused.

Suddenly I recognized what the Devil was attempting to do: pull our family to pieces. "Wait just a second! Shelley is entitled to voice her feelings, even if they're not the same as ours, Chris. Don't you two recognize what's going on here? The Devil would just love to see us turn on each other."

"Divide and conquer—" Chris halted in his tracks. "Right! If we let this fracture our family any more than it already has, there's no way— Well, don't worry, Mom. We'll find strength from the Lord. Somehow we're going to get through this thing."

Shelley stopped combing and primping. Her arm dropped to her side, and she had the grace to look ashamed. "I'm sorry, Mom. I guess I really sounded crass. I care as much as anyone about Scott. I just can't handle it, is all."

I put my arms around her. "Shelley, this is very hard on all of us. If you build a wall around your heart, you'll be shutting all of us out, even the Lord."

Shelley's face crumpled; she curled into herself and buried her face in my neck. "Help me, Mom. The pain is more than I can stand."

Shelley and Scott had been extremely close before all this happened. "Go ahead," I encouraged, my own tears flowing. "Crying is good for us all."

Chris came over, and we all stood with our arms wrapped around each other, bawling. It was the first time we'd been able to unleash our grief together, and it was an important step toward family unity. We had a lot to face together in the months ahead, and we were going to need each other's support.

Chapter 6. Facing the Music

We finally reached Scott's attorney, Mr. Irving, the next morning at eight. Scott's court appearance was scheduled for nine, and we had already told him the night before to waive extradition, as Office Schneider had suggested.

However, after talking with Mr. Irving, we came to see that waiving extradition meant Scott could languish in a jail cell for as long as thirty days before Idaho sent a deputy to accompany him back to face charges in Boise. In the meantime, he would be rubbing shoulders with hardened criminals and possibly experience sexual abuse, beatings or worse. Scott had expressed a desire to face the Boise authorities as soon as possible; he wanted to get the whole mess out in the open.

Mr. Irving promised he would try to contact Scott before he got into the courtroom and advise him *not* to waive extradition. Then Scott could be released on bail, and he could turn himself in under our custody to the Idaho authorities.

The night before, I had visited Scott in the County jail.

I had questioned him about what Detective Schneider told us. "What about stealing gas in Pioche, Scott?" I queried.

Scott wasn't especially talkative or cooperative. I sensed he was worried that our conversation was being monitored or taped by the police. After all, we were speaking through phones, with a heavy glass barrier between. I decided not to get too specific. I didn't want to say anything that would prevent Scott from getting a fair trial.

"Mom, if I had stolen all the stuff they say, why didn't the police find it when they stopped me? They even searched the truck cab," he said, grinning.

"That's an interesting point," I agreed. "I don't t know if you realize how lucky you are to be alive. They had you labeled as 'armed and extremely dangerous.' They could have shot you on sight anywhere between Boise and Phoenix."

"You worry too much, Mom. Besides, nothing can kill me until it's my time to die."

I winced at his callous sounding attitude. "Scott, you need to cooperate with the police. You must know something about what happened up there in Idaho. Why take the rap for the Bakers? They obviously set you up." I caught myself; I was starting to sound like the hard-boiled detective in a Sue Grafton novel. I dropped the subject and began urging Scott to put his faith in the Lord and turn State's evidence. I knew he wasn't being truthful with me; he had to know more than he was willing to admit.

"Mom, you and Dad are working yourself into such a stew over this. I tell you, they haven't a shred of evidence against me," he insisted.

"If you say so." I sighed. "Do you need anything? Have you talked to Linda today? "

"No, but we spoke on the phone. She's pretty worried about things, but I'm okay. I just want out of this stinking hole. They have murderers and rapists in here, big time."

He moved about restlessly.

"Have you had a shower since you've been in here, Scott?" I asked, noticing how sweaty he looked.

"Are you kidding?" He looked at me as if I came from another planet. "The showers aren't safe, unless you want some queer—"

"Scott! Watch your language," I protested. "You really have a dirty mouth."

"Hey, that's nothing compared to what goes on in here, especially at night." He shrugged. "I hardly get any sleep at all in here. This other guy and I stand guard so we can catch a few winks. Otherwise, we might get jumped by some weirdo."

"Scott, I promise, we're going to get you out of here as soon as we can."

"Everything's going to be cool, Mom. I just need to get up to Idaho and straighten this whole mess out." Scott seemed in earnest, and he was, for once, looking me straight in the eye. I had a flash of hope: Maybe this was merely a case of his having been "framed." Certainly none of the "facts" presented to us in the Marshall's office and by Detective Schneider sounded like our Scott.

"Just waive extradition, Scott. We'll have you up in Idaho in no time," I had urged the night before his court appearance.

"Right. No sweat."

We said goodnight, and I was let out of the area by the deputy. *What a dreary series of cement corridors with steel doors*, I thought, as I walked out into the night. I hoped Scott would learn his lesson from all this.

The next morning, in case Mr. Irving didn't get hold of Scott, we put a call in to the jail and asked to speak with him. We were told he was already being shipped by bus to the courthouse. We'd been told the arraignment process would be quick, and there was no point in our being in the courtroom.

In fact, there was a good possibility that we wouldn't be admitted. All we could do was pray.

As it turned out, neither Mr. Irving nor our message, sent via the jailer, reached Scott. However, the Lord must have intervened, for Scott, not understanding the judge's question about extradition, refused to waive extradition! This meant we could proceed to arrange his release through Mr. Irving. Because we had owned our own home for several years, we didn't have to post bail. Scott was released on his own recognizance.

That afternoon, Scott and his father returned home around three. Scott was drenched in sweat from head to toe. His long hair was plastered to his head, hanging limp and stringy around his neck. His clothes smelled of filth. Even so, I reached up and hugged him fiercely.

"Welcome home, Scott," I said. I was so glad he wasn't in jail. I had taken the day off for a "family emergency." It was important to use the time to best advantage, so while Scott showered, I went to the telephone.

My telephone call was patched directly to the District Attorney's office in Boise. When his secretary came on the line, she said he was too busy to talk to anyone. Then she asked my name.

I said, "This is Scott Patterson's mother."

Immediately her voice changed. She put me through without delay.

The D.A.'s voice was energized with excitement and fast paced, as he came on the line. "Mrs. Patterson? This is Burl Simms."

I got right to the point. "Mr. Simms, Scott wants to turn himself in. He says he had nothing to do with those burglaries."

Simms then asked, "Has he waived extradition?"

"No," I replied. "We were advised by our attorney down

here that Scott might spend a month or more in jail, awaiting extradition. Scott wants to come see you, now that he's out on his own recognizance."

"That can be arranged. If he can get here within two days, and if his fingerprints don't match prints taken from a door knob, there's a good chance he will just walk away from here, totally clean."

A gust of air left my lungs in relief. "Thank you. Now, if we take him across the Arizona state line, so he can turn himself in up in Idaho, will he be charged with violation of—" I didn't know exactly what words to use. "In other words, Scott doesn't want to break the law getting there."

"There will be no legal recriminations if he turns himself in up here immediately."

I turned to my husband, who was now standing at my side. "Glenn, the District Attorney says Scott has to be in his office in Boise within two days."

Glenn took the receiver. "Mr. Simms, this is Scott's father. I personally guarantee he'll be there, if we have to drive non-stop. All I ask is that he get a fair hearing."

"You've got a deal." Mr. Simms sounded as eager as we were to get the case resolved.

By this time, Chris and Shelley were clustered around the telephone, listening avidly to every word. Glenn hung up and turned to us. "Let's hope Scott is as innocent as he claims. He and I start first thing in the morning."

Chris volunteered, "I'll come with you and Scott, if you want."

"No, son." Glenn shook his head. "This is something Scott must face by himself. I have to go along, because I'm responsible for his whereabouts."

Just then Scott emerged from the bathroom, wrapped in a terry robe. He looked a lot better than when I'd first greeted him at the front door. Even so, he was tense, and there was a scary look in his eyes I'd never seen before.

"You okay, Scott?" Glenn asked, putting his hand on Scott's shoulder.

"Sure, Dad. I heard. Guess I'd better pack." He went down the hall to his room.

Shelley looked after her brother's disappearing back. "He sure seems nervous, Dad. Do you think he's guilty?"

Glenn shook his head. "I don't know. I pray this experience will make a man out of Scott. Up to now, he's treated life pretty much like a game. Maybe he'll have to go to jail for a time, but whatever happens, let's try to be loving and supportive."

Shelley sighed. "I know, Dad. Mom had this same talk with us earlier."

The next morning Glenn and Scott set out after our family had prayer together. Scott "spaced" us a little during devotions, but he needed our help, so he tolerated us as we committed him and the journey to the Lord.

It took two days of steady driving to reach a small motel on the outskirts of Boise.

The next morning, Scott was taken into custody the instant he walked into the District Attorney's office and identified himself. A hubbub of excitement surrounded his "capture," Glenn related to me later. After Scott was booked, fingerprinted and conducted to a jail cell, the waiting began.

After about four hours in the lock-up, he had a surprise visit from the Bakers. As he later told his father, the Bakers, both out on bail, hoped to persuade him to keep quiet about what he knew. Evidently they'd been implicated in a number of crimes. Since they were responsible for Scott's arrest, it was hardly surprising that he wasn't overjoyed to see them. After a few minutes they left, and Scott continued to wait until he could be arraigned and a trial date set.

In the meantime, Glenn secured the name of an outstanding attorney whom the court could assign as Scott's public defender, since we were hardly in a position to pay for a trial lawyer.

The next morning Scott was arraigned before the Grand Jury on one count of burglary. His fingerprints matched a thumb print on a merchant's doorknob. Since the trial wouldn't begin for nearly three months, Scott was again released into his father's custody without bail being set. He and Glenn visited the defending attorney in his office. There Scott received sound advice about being completely candid and not trying to fabricate any alibis, etc. Then he and Glenn drove the grueling long miles home to wait out the time until his case came to trial.

Chapter 7. A Dark Shadow Hangs Over Us All.

Life didn't change much after Glenn and Scott returned from Boise. Scott was on edge and frequently used foul language as a release mechanism. He still came and went with his scroungy friends, although we managed to keep track of him most of the time.

One thing was different: On his "best" behavior, he slept at home every night. After nearly two years of sporadic disappearances and overnighters with friends, this was a relief to us, since we had to account for his whereabouts.

Scott began to lose weight. For the first time in years, he wasn't hungry. He didn't want to talk about what had happened either. As an attorney's daughter, I wanted to know details and hoped to find "loopholes" which would help the defense. As a mother, my energies were consumed with a desire to see Scott set free, if at all possible.

I still prayed the Lord would change Scott's heart. Although I wanted justice to be served, there was a battle raging inside me. I knew from Scott's description of the jail that prison could make a person worse than he were when he went in. I was fearful that he might end up dead, or hardened forever against the Lord and society. My protective maternal instincts were often at war with my faith.

Wrestling with this conflict, I probed for answers that might explain away Scott's involvement with the Bakers. Usually Scott concluded our conversations with anger and rejection. He didn't want to face what had happened in Boise, he would scream, using as much profanity as he thought it would take to get me off his back. He was going through his own struggles, I knew.

Unwilling to regard himself as "criminal," he also didn't want his mother acting like an assistant defense attorney. Yet I saw so many inconsistencies between what the Marshal's office, the detective at the County jail, and the District Attorney's office in Boise said that my mind, grasping for details and the truth, sought to build a logical explanation for why he was on the scene of the burglary. Scott's anger and his apparent eagerness to get through the trial and take whatever punishment was meted out frustrated me.

Two days after Scott returned home with his father, Glenn and I were just sitting down at the dinner table with Chris and Shelley, when the doorbell rang.

We found a large stocky policeman standing in the doorway. He seemed highly excited, which took us by surprise. "Is Scott Patterson home?" he demanded.

"No," said Glenn, coming up behind me and putting an arm around my shoulders. "What can we do for you?"

He cleared his throat. "He and some other kids were seen drag-racing up and down the football field. From the janitor's description, we traced the license to him at this address."

"Scott isn't here right now, Officer. How much damage

has been done to the school grounds?" Though shocked by this latest escapade, Glen didn't dispute the policeman's word.

"Hard to say. Well, if he comes in, please call us at this number," the policeman said, handing his card to Glenn.

Stunned, Glenn and I looked at each other. Once the door was closed, we held a quick family conference. Shelley had to leave for the library to complete some research on a term paper, Chris opted to stay by the telephone, in case Scott called in.

Meanwhile Glenn and I got into our station wagon and started out. Our first thought was that Scott might have gone over to his girl friend's house, so we drove there, a distance of perhaps four miles. The house was dark; clearly, the family wasn't at home. Scott, however, was standing in the driveway, leaning against the side of his truck, smoking a joint and laughing raucously with two other young males. His girl friend Linda wasn't present.

We drove in behind his truck and got out.

"Scott, can we talk to you?" Glenn began.

Scott spotted us, and his eyes blazed with hostility. "Get away from me!" he screamed. "Clear out, or I'll—" His voice rose as he unleashed a tirade of threats and profanity.

Neither of us budged. "Scott, the police came to the house. They say you were driving all over the football field. Is that true?"

"None of your business!" he yelled, obviously trying to impress his friends with how tough he was. If he hadn't had an audience, we felt it would have been easier to talk to him.

Glenn walked over and tried to put his arm around Scott.

He wrenched himself away. The sickening stench of marijuana smoke drifted in the air.

"Get away from me, old man!"

"Take it easy, Scott. We just wanted to warn you. The police are out looking for you. The last thing you need right now is another arrest, especially when you're high."

"Later," Scott snarled and got into his truck. Revving up the engine, he yelled, "Pile in, guys. Let's space these two squares." He turned himself around on the semi-circular drive, tires spinning gravel.

"Scott, listen to us. You're high, and you shouldn't be driving," I said, stepping into the beam of his headlights.

"Move it, you meddling old woman, or I'll mow you down—Dad, too. You're always interfering. Always giving me a hard time." He moved his truck forward, racing his motor menacingly.

I stepped aside and returned to our car. Glenn got in on the driver's side. "Scott, I wish you would listen," I tried again.

This time he hit our car a thud on the bumper.

"Get out!" he bellowed.

"There's no reasoning with him," Glenn said and moved our car back quickly to avoid another collision.

Scott pealed out of Linda's driveway with his friends. His truck was weaving unsteadily as he drove down the street at breakneck speed. We followed him a short distance, but there was no keeping up with him without taking our lives in our hands.

Glenn looked haggard. I could tell his heart was broken. As a young child, Scott had been the apple of his father's eye, and he had always looked forward to enjoying a closer relationship with him when he grew older. Somehow, Scott had never been interested in sharing the same experiences with Glenn that Chris did. Camping, boating, hiking—these were too "tame" for Scott, our daredevil. From an early age, he preferred being out with his peers, hanging around at their houses and swapping tall tales.

"Glenn, don't take it so hard," I consoled, moving toward him on the front seat. "I guess he's going to have to learn everything the hard way."

"I feel so helpless, Sandy." His voice broke. "He's bent on destroying himself, and I can't even figure out why!" He hit the steering wheel with his palm. "Why, Lord? *Why?*"

I sat silently beside him. Then an idea occurred to me. "Glenn, why don't we go over to the football stadium and see what kind of damage Scott did? After all, he doesn't have a job, and we're probably going to be asked to make restitution."

Reluctantly he agreed, and we drove over. When we got there, we spotted Ernie, one of Scott's "druggy" friends, next to a patrol car with its lights rotating. Ernie was standing beside his bicycle, his hands in cuffs, talking to the officer, who was patting him down.

"Ernie," I said, getting out of the car. "What's going on? Have you seen Scott?"

"Maybe about an hour ago," he replied. "Before he got chased off by some old man. We were having a great time out there on the football field."

"You forgot to mention he was driving his truck," Glenn said with a touch of irony in his voice.

"What's Ernie done, Officer?" I asked, turning to the policeman.

"He's the neighborhood pusher, ma'am. I pat him down routinely. Caught with the goods this time," he added, holding up a plastic bag with brownish weed. "Hashish."

We identified ourselves and inquired into the ruckus our son had created earlier. When the patrolman heard Scott's name, his interest heightened. "Scott Patterson? We have ten patrol cars and a police helicopter out looking for him right now. The kid's 'armed and dangerous.'"

"Scott isn't armed. He's high as a kite on marijuana, but he doesn't have a gun," Glenn said forcefully.

"That sounds like what they said when he was arrested awhile back," I realized with a shock. I broke out in a cold sweat; the thought of Scott being gunned down made every

nerve in my body tense with fear. "He's *never* had a gun.
Please check that computer of yours, Officer. I believe that
information goes back to his arrest nearly two weeks ago."

The policeman looked at us, and Glenn pressed for his
cooperation. "Please check downtown headquarters. I'd hate
to see the police department make a fatal mistake and shoot an
unarmed man."

The policeman nodded. Perhaps our earnestness convinced him to check into the matter, rather than just accept the
police scanner's word for it. He contacted the dispatcher by
radio, and soon we heard confirmation that the "scope" still
carried the warning that Scott was "armed and dangerous."

"That means they'd be justified to shoot him on sight," he
told us reluctantly.

By now, I was shaking visibly. "Officer, I'm not leaving
here until this mistake gets straightened out. Please have them
contact Boise's police department. That information must be
removed from the 'scope'—right now!

Glenn started talking to Ernie, while the patrolman
conveyed our concern about Scott's safety to his supervisor.
We stood talking under the stadium lights for nearly forty-five
minutes before the dispatcher finally called back to let us know
the information had been corrected.

Thanking the patrolman for his assistance, we then
arranged with Ernie to return his bicycle to his mother's house.
Already in the patrol car, he asked us to let her know about his
arrest. We drove slowly down the block with Ernie's bicycle
on the luggage rack of our station wagon. During our visit
with Ernie's sister, we got a sample of what we had to look
forward to as parents of a felon.

As we brought the bicycle up to the door, Ernie's sister
answered the doorbell. "Hi. Thanks for bringing Ernie's bike
home," she said. "Care to come in?"

We declined. "Sorry, but we need to be getting home.

We just wanted to drop off his bike and let you know he's been arrested for possession of marijuana."

She shook her head. "Again? Oh, well, that's no surprise."

"Can we do anything to help? Glenn asked.

"No. Boy, this will just kill Mother when she hears about it, though. This is the third time this month he's been busted."

"I'm sorry to hear you've had so much trouble," I said. "It must be very hard on the family."

"Hard!" She uttered a snort. "My Mom and Dad have ruined their health worrying about Ernie. He's wiped out their savings. They can plead and talk a blue streak, but nothing ever changes. He just turns a deaf ear and gets loaded."

Glenn handed her his church calling card. "I have a son, a friend of Ernie's, who's having problems, too. If I can ever help you or your parents, please contact me."

The sister stared down at the card. "Maybe if Mom and Dad had called a minister ten years ago, it would have done some good. It's probably too late now."

Glenn smiled reassuringly. "Without faith, it's easy to think that, but it's never too late. Have your parents call me, if they need to talk to someone. It helps to share burdens."

She seemed visibly touched by his concern. "Thanks," she said. "Maybe it *would* help the pain go away a little. I'll tell my parents you stopped by."

Within the next two weeks, that contact seeded a support group for hurting families of teenagers in trouble with the law. We weren't exactly thrilled at the circumstances that led to our involvement, but we derived some comfort in being able to share our faith, which had sustained us thus far.

Even so, we knew Scott had a long road to travel ahead of him.

Chapter 8. *Where Did It All Begin?*

As we waited anxiously through the next couple of months before the trial, there was plenty of time for soul searching and agonizing over the past. Glenn and I spent many nights tossing and turning, praying, and sometimes, mentally bashing ourselves for failing to keep Scott out of trouble.

Eighteen years before, nobody could have been happier than Glenn when Scott was born. Although he was thrilled with the miracle of Shelley's birth, he was *ecstatic* when Scott made his entrance into the world the following year. Here was the son he'd always dreamed of sharing "man things" with.

As a baby, Scott was cheerful and easy to love. He was also surprising active. At twelve months, he managed to climb from his high chair onto the top of the refrigerator. He couldn't walk yet, but from that moment on, we had cause to worry about his tendency to be a daredevil.

My worst fright came when he was three, and I came upon him perched on the second story balcony railing of our house. Below, a neighbor was trying to talk him out of "stunt flying" from the balcony with his kite. I was petrified, knowing that the slightest sudden move might startle him and cause him to fall. Talking quietly, I moved in slowly—it felt like an eternity!—until I was close enough to make a quick grab and scoop him into my arms.

Scott was more physical than his sister Shelley, who later developed into an excellent student. I had some concern about how well a hyperactive child would do in school, but for the most part, he was a loving, responsive child, so I decided I was worrying unduly.

Our family life was unremarkable until about the time Glenn assumed a new pastorate in Colorado. Shortly after Scott's fifth birthday, we packed up our small brood, which included Chris by this time. In the small ranching community we were called to serve, the next three years were great fun for us as a family. However, a few warning signs began to surface.

About two years after we moved to Colorado, we went on a camping trip with another church family. While hiking, Scott tripped over a tree root and tumbled headlong down an embankment, striking his head on a fallen log. He lay there momentarily stunned, then got to his feet unsteadily. Soon he was vomiting, and other symptoms of concussion quickly followed.

Frightened, I propped Scott up in the car while Glenn drove down the mountain to the nearest doctor. Chris and Shelley were ashen-faced as they held their brother's hand in the waiting room. He was still retching, and his eyes were unfocused.

Glenn breathed a prayer as we waited. Although it seemed forever, the nurse took us back to an examination room in only a few minutes. The doctor admitted Scott overnight to the hospital and with the use of steroids and close surveillance, he was soon able to return home. We were warned to be on the lookout for any recurring physical symptoms, including signs of a personality change.

It was nearly a month before he was strong enough to resume his usual pursuits. During his recuperation, he was especially cooperative, but didn't want me to leave his side even for a minute. The extra attention he received while out of school appealed to him. After awhile I decided he was "milking" the situation.

Once I stopped waiting on him, he quickly became his old rambunctious self, with one slight difference: He began bringing home small items from local stores without paying for them. Because some of the store owners were church members, they tried to spare our feelings by not telling us. We first learned through church gossip that Scott was shoplifting.

Both Glenn and I took strong measures as soon as we

recognized there was a problem. However, Scott continued to defy us. He tried to cover up his actions by lying. Even when punished or placed on restriction, he persisted in lying, often about the most obvious and unnecessary things.

About this time, sibling rivalry began to influence his attitude toward his brother Chris. I found myself constantly having to separate them to keep Scott from inflicting physical harm on his brother.

Shelley, who seemed to revel in intrigue, kept Scott stirred up in quiet conspiracies. In her own way, she encouraged him to pit his will against his parents. This marked the beginning of a power struggle. Naturally, Scott wound up receiving more than his share of the blame, while Shelley sat back, smiling like the proverbial Cheshire cat. Later, she would commiserate with him, but somehow she managed to escape punishment herself.

Another change occurred in our family situation during that pastorate which shook the foundation of Scott's security. Due to finances, I was forced to work outside the home to help meet expenses. Scott's reaction was volatile. He began to act out. He even went so far as to "lose" his brother Chris in an old abandoned house on the outskirts of town. We located Chris only after we had "grilled" Scott for hours. What a relief, when we finally found Chris, who had spent the time alternately reading old comic books and exploring the dilapidated old house.

Shortly thereafter, Scott dropped by the store where I was busy waiting on customers behind the counter. He managed to swipe several items. When I discovered them under his bed at home, he readily admitted where they came from. "Now you'll have to stay home with me," he told me.

"Why do you think that?" I asked, studying his face.

He smiled in triumph. "You'll lose your job when we take everything back to Mr. Tate." It was obvious he had no concept of how hard pressed we were financially.

""You *wanted* to get caught stealing, didn't you?" I was angry that he thought he could manipulate me into staying home. "Well, let me tell you, Scott Patterson. I am not working away from home because I want to. Our family has bills to pay, and right now that means Daddy and I both have to work. Do you understand?"

"I don't care. I want you home. Mothers are supposed to be home when their kids get back from school."

He hadn't heard a word I said!

We returned the items to Mr. Tate, who sat Scott down and tried to acquaint him with the fact that stealing was wrong. Again, Scott seemed impervious to every argument. He just knew what *he* wanted, and nothing else seemed important but to get his own way.

Meanwhile even his "conspirator" Shelley starting having her problems with Scott. At times things backfired, as he vented his tantrums on her.

Pitting his wits and wry humor against Scott's superior brawn, Chris came under attack as well. Scott resented Chris's quick wit and status as the youngest member of the family. He had a difficult time disguising his animosity. Not that Chris was altogether innocent; he often said things to provoke Scott's outbursts. Naturally, Scott got into trouble when he lashed out with his fists.

Meanwhile Glenn's ministry was flourishing. Soon his successes received enough recognition that by the end of our third year, we found ourselves moving again, this time to Phoenix. We hoped the change might help Scott feel more secure and that this would be reflected in his behavior.

Whatever aspirations I had of resuming the role of resident mother were soon frustrated. Even though I was now home, Scott was already busy cooking up trouble with the neighbors. He had a talent for stirring up dissension with other children. He was always racing in the front door with an irate kid on his tail.

When we had a chance to sell the house, we moved a couple of miles closer to Glenn's church. We sensed that we were rapidly approaching a family crisis because of Scott's behaviors.

Chapter 9. The Acting Out Continues.

In the fifth grade, Scott got caught smoking marijuana with an older boy in the school bathroom. We took his teacher's advice and enrolled him in a private Christian school. There he was blessed with a tough-minded male teacher, who recognized Scott's need for discipline and provided a physical outlet for his energies. Every time Scott caused a class disruption, didn't complete an assignment on time, or gave his teacher the least bit of backtalk, he was sent out to run laps on the school track.

How he admired his teacher for making him tow the mark! He accepted his discipline cheerfully, and for the next school year, life seemed relatively peaceful.

Our new home was in a developing area with not too many neighbors at first. A few months after we moved in, however, the vacant land mushroomed into a medium income housing tract. That's when the fun really began.

Always gregarious, Scott made instant friends with the new boys in the neighborhood. Before long, it became a common sight to see police cruisers breaking up groups of young "hoodlums," gathered at the bus stop, smoking, and hazing younger kids on their way home from school.

We began to wonder if *all* their parents had moved there for the same reason we had—to get away from problems created by their kids in other neighborhoods!

Back in public school for seventh grade, Scott began playing hookey from school. We became well acquainted with the inside of the principal's office and the dean of students in the weeks that followed.

Then one day, a police detective came to the house. He said he had evidence that Scott and three other boys had broken into a man's house, stolen some potted "flowers"— chrysanthemums, I believe the man said. The boys had broken a brass musical instrument and stolen some *Playboy* magazines. The detective agreed that the man was probably growing marijuana in his pots, but he was still obliged to place Scott under arrest for breaking and entering.

Scott appeared before a juvenile judge with a reputation for being tough but fair. Without blinking, he sentenced our son to six months in a detention center.

Scott, barely thirteen, swayed as if he might faint on the spot. The blood drained from his face, as he managed to utter his plaintive plea, "I can change, your Honor, I promise to change. *Please* don't send me away."

The judge, a formidable black man in a black robe, scowled over his glasses at Scott. "And why should I believe that, young man? How do I know you won't go right back out there and steal again?"

"I'll go to school and quit hanging around with those guys," Scott promised. I felt a little sorry for him. Up until then, I doubted that he realized the seriousness of his actions.

After a stern lecture, the judge suspended the sentence with the words, "Don't *ever* appear before me again, or I won't be so kind."

Scott returned home, and things went a bit more smoothly for awhile. A month before Christmas, his grandmother came to visit, little dreaming what we'd been going through with Scott. Soon, However, she realized that something was desperately wrong.

Two nights after she arrived, one of our neighbors came over, threatening to put Scott in jail for stealing his son's bicycle. We knew no bicycle had turned up at our house, so we had our doubts. However, the man demanded to search our house. Because Glenn is a reasonable man and we wanted to reassure the man, we allowed him to walk through the house and backyard with us. He left, still not convinced, and assured us that we would be hearing from him again.

The next day he was back. This time he claimed Scott had threatened to "blow away" his son with a .357 Magnum. We told him we kept no guns around the house, that the remark, if made, was nothing but an idle threat. The man said he was going to the authorities, since we weren't able to "control" our son.

The next afternoon I came home early from a meeting. Scott and some of his buddies were in the kitchen, frying hamburgers and stirring up a lot of smoke and grease on the stove. Some of his friends looked pretty skinny and probably could use a good meal, so I said nothing about the mess, as I began to prepare supper.

As I moved about my ears began picking up tidbits from their male bragging contest about a "mind blowing" incident at the bus stop after school that day. This was soon confirmed by Chris, when he came in a few minutes later.

It seems that the man who had accused Scott of stealing his son's bicycle had summoned the police and also involved the principal of Scott's school. When the junior high school bus drew up to our neighborhood stop, a block from our house, eight squad cars and a police helicopter, as well as the principal and her aide, were on hand to greet the bus.

When Scott wasn't among the students that poured off the bus, there was a great deal of confused excitement, as several students provided the police with wild descriptions of Scott. Meanwhile Scott, who had played hookey, lounged on top of a short block wall across the street from the bus stop, enjoying the scene as much as any of his friends. All this for his benefit! Thanks to exaggerated reports about what a dangerous person he was (and all those adults believing it), Scott became an instant hero in the eyes of every loser and dropout for blocks around. All the police artillery created a persona for Scott that was hard to shake. He thought it was quite funny.

After the police and school principal waited around for twenty minutes for the notorious gunslinger, Scott sauntered over and asked, "What's happening, Officer?"

"We're looking for Scott Patterson. The kid's armed. Threatened another student." The police officer was pacing grimly, in full riot gear, according to Scott's account.

"I know Scott," Scott told him, straight-faced. "He's not such a bad guy."

"That's not what we heard," the policeman said, taking the bait.

"Yeah, well, I'm Scott Patterson," Scott introduced himself, "and I don't have a gun. This sideshow is sure pretty silly, just because a kid got his butt kicked at school."

The other boy's father stepped forward. He hadn't met Scott personally before. "Who are you, son?" he asked in a friendly manner, evidently hoping to solicit Scott's aid in finding the culprit who had stolen his kid's bicycle.

"I'm Scott Patterson, and your son still sucks his thumb," Scott told him. "I beat him up at school a few days ago, so he hid his bicycle and accused me of stealing it."

The man didn't know what to say. "Well, you leave my son alone, y'hear me?" he said defensively. "I don't want him associating with a rotten kid like you."

"Sure thing, man," Scott shrugged. "No sweat." He ambled off through the crowd, a few of his friends trailing behind him admiringly. They headed right over to our house to celebrate the creation of a new legendary hero.

Naturally I was concerned about the notoriety this incident created for Scott and us as his family. Knowing Scott was anything but an angel, I didn't want to "rock the boat." I dropped the subject and the "legend" continued to haunt us in the days that followed.

You can imagine the children's grandmother's reaction on hearing this! She was a very straight-laced Christian from an era when smoking in the girls' restroom at the local high school was scandalous. I was very surprised that she stayed on through the holidays.

A few days later, she went to Glenn, complaining that ten dollars had disappeared from her purse. A brief investigation revealed the thief. By this time, Glenn was getting "battle fatigue" from the continual problems with Scott. He decided to take Scott down to the Juvenile Detention Hall and turn him in as "unmanageable."

After two days in detention, Scott was assigned to a counselor who was very understanding. Everyone agreed that Scott needed supervision by someone outside the family to whom he reported on a regular basis. Scott was pretty close-mouthed with Glenn and me when we visited him in the detention center. When he appeared before the judge for "stealing from his own grandmother," Scott meekly promised to cooperate and was released into our custody.

"I certainly hope you've learned something from all this, Scott," Glenn said sternly.

Dressed in his suit, Scott looked rather shaken, as if he'd gone through a severe emotional trauma. "Just get me out of here," he said tersely.

Little did we know the impact those two days in detention had had on him. Almost immediately, Scott began to display a hostile edge. He seemed angry and distrustful of authority figures. More and more often, he got "stoned" and stayed out late with friends. Even at noon, it wasn't unusual to see his eyes glazed, his pupils dilated. We found pot smoking paraphernalia and cigarette papers and realized he was delving deeper into drugs. We found pornographic magazines under his bed; repeatedly we threw them away or burned them, only to see more lurid publications appear.

Here was a thirteen-year-old boy letting his hair grow longer and longer, refusing to bathe or change his clothes, stalking in and out of our house with his friends, cursing and generally making our lives miserable. We were frightened to think where he would wind up if he continued on this way. We tried to discourage his hanging out with his friends, but our pleas seemed only to inspire more anti-social behavior.

We were losing the battle.

Over the next few months the situation became even more tense. It became impossible to invite Christian friends to the house, because they and we were almost certain to be subjected to verbal abuse by Scott, as he sank deeper into the dark world of drugs, alcohol and delinquency.

At age fifteen, Scott had his first serious infatuation with a girl. He had developed into a handsome, rather dashing figure looked up to among his peers. Since age fourteen, he'd had a bevy of girls competing for his attention, but from the moment he and Tina met, things clicked.

Immediately we saw a difference. Scott began to bathe twice daily. He ran through several clean shirts a day, occasionally consented to a haircut, and began holding long conversations with Tina on the telephone. This was so "normal" for teenagers that we were encouraged to believe perhaps he would abandon his wild habits. Our prayer was that he would ditch his pot smoking pals and take a real interest in his studies, since his girl friend was a good student.

Everything went along fairly peacefully for about four months. Long enough for the family to relax our guard and start enjoying Scott's more winning characteristics.

Suddenly Tina's parents were in the throes of a divorce, and Tina reacted by breaking off her friendship with Scott. Scott's reaction hit without warning, like an avalanche tearing down a slope on a cloudless day. He ditched first period and showed up, sobbing inconsolably, at the office, where I was now working as an insurance claims adjuster. It was obvious that he had genuine feelings for Tina, even though they were both so young. I tried to reassure him that even though breaking up was painful, it wasn't the end of the world. He finally left, and I went back to processing insurance claims.

Two hours later, Glenn called to let me know Scott had been arrested with two friends for drunkenness. Leaving my office, he has run into two classmates. They had "found" a bottle of whiskey and were sitting on a curb when a patrol car pulled up and took them into custody. Glenn went down and picked Scott up from detention an hour later. Charges were dropped for "insufficient evidence." We were relieved to learn that Scott wasn't legally drunk. [I think his probation officer was, too.] He claimed he had just accompanied the other boys to make sure they made it safely home. How we wanted to believe his story.

At nine that evening, Glenn was reading in the den and I was putting away dishes when a knock summoned me to the front door. Standing there, filling the doorway with his bulk was one of Scott's disheveled buddies, Ted.

The look on his face touched off an instant alarm inside me. "What's wrong, Ted?" I asked, already taking off my apron. I knew something serious was up.

"Scott's out in the park under a tree. He's trying to kill himself with a broken bottle. I think you and Reverend Patterson better come quick." Ted looked genuinely scared.

"Glenn!" I yelled. "Come quick! Scott's trying to kill himself!" I grabbed my purse and car keys.

Glenn came up from his book in a hurry. His face had a

haunted look as he moved toward the door, pulling on his jacket. "Where is he, Ted?" he demanded.

We jumped in the car with Ted, a heavyset tall teenager crowding the two or us in the front seat.

"He's at the back of the park where there aren't any lights. He's had a lot to drink, and I think he got some Quaalude from Eric's mom. She gave him a bottle of wine, too."

Glenn pulled out of our driveway and wheeled out of the cul-de-sac we lived on, tires screeching. I noticed that his temples were turning grey.

Ted directed us toward the dark side of the public park nearby. We could make out Scott's silhouette dimly. He was sitting on the ground, his back against a tree. Two boys were hunched over him, trying to reason with him.

"Leave me alone," Scott wept. "I wanna die! I'm nothing but trouble. Nobody cares what happens to me anyway." His tone took on more anger as he continued to rave. He kept jabbing at his wrists with a jagged piece of broken glass. He had cut himself, but was in no immediate danger of bleeding to death.

Ignoring Scott's protests, Ted and Glenn hauled him to his feet and started dragging him toward the car. I slid behind the steering wheel, while Ted pushed Scott into the back seat beside him. Glenn got in back on the other side, blocking Scott from escape.

The other boys left as soon as they knew Scott wasn't going to do himself harm. Despite their bad habits and reputation for experimenting with drugs, I felt a certain gratitude for their looking out for Scott. They could have walked away and left him out there alone. In the dark, no one would have known his predicament. By morning, Scott might have succeeded in carrying out his threat of self-destruction.

"Drive to the emergency room, Sandy." Glenn put his arms around Scott's heaving shoulders. Scott was sobbing uncontrollably and striking the back of my seat with his fists. Occasionally he hit himself in the head, as he cursed and thrashed about. Ted tried to talk to him, but soon gave up when Scott started getting abusive.

"Stop the car, Mom," Scott screamed. "Let me out of here!"

"No, Scott, I won't," I said in an even voice. "I *can't*. You need help. How much drugs and alcohol have you had tonight?" I could have strangled his friend Eric's mother for supplying the neighborhood kids with Quaaludes and wine.

"None of your business. You and Dad will only 'narc' to the cops again." Scott seemed fairly lucid, but his emotional state worried us.

At the emergency room, we were met by an indifferent nurse, who showed a total lack of concern for Scott's predicament and the other people waiting to be seen. One man was having a seizure from a drug overdose not fifteen feet from her station. I couldn't believe a nurse could get so "burned out" that she didn't bat an eye or take steps to help the man.

After a short wait, Glenn decided we should leave and try another hospital nearby. When we got there, Glenn explained to the staff, who seemed more responsive, that Scott had been threatening suicide after ingesting alcohol and drugs. The doctor came out and recommended keeping Scott overnight in the psychiatric ward, so he could be evaluated when he was more coherent.

The words "stay overnight" sent Scott rocketing to his feet. He dashed out the door and in one bound, leapt on top of a six foot block wall fence in the parking lot. He cat-walked along the top of the fence in the cold night air, cursing and shouting at the top of his lungs. Once again, he accused us of trying to "get rid" of him and of not caring. He seemed to regard us as his enemies.

Everything we did was interpreted as interference and

rejection. We couldn't understand how he had gotten this picture of us in his head, when we were trying in every way to demonstrate our concern and love. He even accused us of "adopting" him, a preposterous idea, and said maybe that was why we "hated" him so much.

A hospital security guard had followed us into the parking lot, but we assured him we didn't need his help. We were afraid Scott would become even more out of control, if too many people became involved.

Finally, a young woman from a local crisis hotline was able to get him calmed down a bit. It was nearly three in the morning by this time, and we were greatly relieved to see the effects of alcohol and drugs wearing off. Scott was becoming calmer, more coherent. After getting us to promise not to put him in the hospital, he finally came down off the fence and talked for awhile with the young woman counselor.

Around four in the morning, we drove home from the hospital and dragged ourselves, exhausted, off to bed. Two hours later, Glenn got up for a six o'clock prayer breakfast. Meanwhile Scott slept until noon, oblivious of the toll his behavior had taken on the rest of his family.

Chapter 10. Out of Control.

I have no idea how Scott passed the Ninth Grade. In Tenth Grade, unfortunately, he traveled with a pack who skipped class, smoked pot, swapped lies, and generally made life miserable for the security guards who patrolled the school grounds.

Scott was considered a ringleader, a trouble-maker. His reputation, some of it undeserved, most of it earned, had followed him from junior high school. The school kept a close eye on the Patterson's "bad boy."

Two months into the school year, Scott had a run-in with

a security guard at a football game. Scott mouthed off and the security guard tried to throw him out of the stadium. In the scuffle, Scott managed to deliver a few strategic punches and kicks to the groin.

Once again I found myself in the school counselor's office with Scott at my side. The security guard came in and seeing Scott, left the room. A minute later, the counselor picked up the telephone. Immediately we realized that the police had been summoned, and the security guard intended to press charges. Scott took off on foot, proving once again what an athlete he was, even if he had never pulled down more than a "C" in P.E.

After Scott disappeared, the counselor called the security guard back into the office. Together they told me that if Scott never returned to the school campus, they would drop the charges. Since Scott didn't like school and was making no effort, I promised we would help him find a job and see that he got counseling, which seemed higher priorities at the moment anyway.

The counselor thanked me, adding, "Mrs. Patterson, you're a good person. I hope for your sake Scott straightens up. Right now, I wouldn't give him a prayer."

Two hours later, Scott showed up at my office, still upset. We both agreed that he should find a job and forget school for awhile.

To my relief, Scott found work right away as a construction worker. He started out at ten dollars an hour, and we were really pleased when we began to hear glowing reports from his employer about how well he was doing. Everyone on the job seemed to value his hard working attitude.

Soon Scott was promoted to fourteen dollars an hour! He was quick to pick up on how things should be done. Once he was shown a task, he had no difficulty performing the work, even improving on what he'd been taught.

The new respect he enjoyed as a wage-earning "adult" gave his self-esteem a boost. Again, we were encouraged to hope. His attitude was such a contrast to his resentment of his teachers. I began to see that much of Scott's behavior stemmed from his struggle to be accepted and treated as an adult. Authority figures at school and, I confess, at home, only inspired him to rebellion. Working for the Yankee dollar seemed to establish him, in his own eyes at least, as a man.

At any rate, he was very highly regarded on the job. Never a moment of trouble, we were told.

Earning all that money was a pretty "heady" experience for Scott. He went through hundreds of dollars without blinking. He bought a used truck, and he and his buddies spent every spare moment rebuilding or replacing everything under the hood. Evenings, they either "crashed" or "got high," depending on which substance they were abusing. It was no secret that every convenience store was "easy" for teens to buy beer.

Despite the dissipation, he never missed a day's work. He started work at six in the morning and got off around two-thirty, which meant he had a lot of time to "hang out" with his buddies at the school bus stop. He was sixteen and even a man's job didn't interfere with "checking out the chicks." Soon he had a string of girl friends, whom he treated like possessions. It was part of maintaining his image among the neighborhood males.

Most of the time, Scott managed to avoid physical altercations. He made plenty of verbal threats, and generally his blustering swagger faked rivals into backing off. Finally he mouthed off once too often, and another boy called his bluff.

They traded punches, and in the process, Scott broke his hand. Although he managed to retain his "turf" and the esteem of his peers and girl friends, he was out of work for six weeks, due to the cast on his hand and arm.

Never handling leisure well, Scott "cruised" the neighborhood, bored. Two weeks later, I received a phone call from Chris at my office.

"They've got Scott," he told me without preamble.

"Who? Who's got Scott? What are you talking about, Chris?" I demanded, trying to shift gears from my work as an insurance adjuster to the role of mother/trouble shooter.

"The cops. Scott was hanging out at the bus stop when he got into an argument with some drunk old lady who came to pick up her kid. She threw vodka and orange juice in his face—*honest!* I saw it, Mom," Chris verified. "Anyway, he started cussing and called her some bad names. Then a guy came out of his house and started after Scott. That's when Scott pulled a knife out of his pocket. He looked scared, Mom. I guess he thought the guy was going to jump him."

I closed my eyes, not wanting to hear. *Oh, Lord, what next?* I thought.

"Anyway, this cop car came around the corner, and the man called him over. He said Scott was trying to kill him. It wasn't true, Mom! I saw what was going on, really!"

"Never mind, Chris. Just stick to the story." I could just see Scott, trying to act brave when he wasn't, and pulling a pocket knife to bolster his courage.

"The cop patted him down and found a small bag of marijuana in his jeans pocket, Mom. He arrested Scott for carrying a concealed weapon and possession of a controlled substance." Chris's voice broke. "Mom, they have Scott down at Juvy."

"Okay. Right after work I'll go down there and see what's going on. Meanwhile, call your father. Just once, Chris, couldn't you call your father first?" I complained. I hung up the phone and put my head in my hands. I thought, *This is the last straw. I can't take any more.*

I finished up the afternoon's work. I doubt anyone at work even knew anything out of the ordinary was going on in our family. But deep inside, every time I got one of these phone calls, the wound went deeper. I was at the point where even the sound of a police siren, or the sight of a young person pulled over to the side of the road by a police car made my heart leap in my throat. There was always that fear in the back of my mind that Scott might be the one who had been stopped. Instead of the police making me feel secure, I found myself consumed with fear. I was afraid for Scott, so afraid. He turned a deaf ear to our counsel, but that didn't lessen my anxiety or pain.

After work I drove directly to Juvenile Detention. I signed Scott out, promising to appear with him in court in one month, and we drove home in silence. I didn't want to launch into a tirade. I was worn out. Besides, nagging accomplished nothing.

All the way home, Scott kept trying to justify himself, telling me he didn't even know the marijuana was there in his pocket, that it was less than an eighth of an ounce. With his broken hand, he said there was "no way" he could have gotten it out of his pocket anyway. I had to agree with him that the cast on his hand did make getting into a tight jean pocket difficult, if not impossible. But the fact that it was there could not be ignored. I knew we were looking at more legal fees for Scott's defense.

Glenn was busy ironing out some problems with one of his church boards, so he was able to give Scott's latest escapade only minimal attention. He was visibly upset, but the burden of dealing with Scott and keeping him in line fell to me. I felt as though Satan was using Scott's immaturity and Glenn's heavy schedule to drive a wedge between us.

Meanwhile Scott continued to demonstrate his inde-pendence by waging a one-sided war against his family, the "fuzz," and "old fogey" neighbors. It seemed that Scott's only allies in this war were his deadbeat friends; their opinion mattered; ours apparently didn't.

Chris and Shelley's responses to this family schism were totally different. Shelley drifted into spending more and more time with her circle of friends at church and school. Embarrassed by Scott's anti-social behaviors, she found it easier to blank out what was going on and renewed her efforts to raise scholarship funds for an out-of-state college. Even so, she was vocal in her resentment that so much of our energies were lavished on Scott. I can't say I blamed her. There were plenty of times I wanted to run away, too.

Chris, quiet and sensitive, found himself cast in the difficult role of comforter. Because of his unusual maturity, he was often treated more like a friend and confidant than a child. I found myself thanking God for his sensible behavior. I don't know what I would have done if I'd had more than one "bad egg" on my hands. Looking back, I wonder if this exalted expectation of Chris didn't place an unreasonable burden on him, although he never complained.

Meanwhile Glenn and I were both experiencing "burn out." Scott had done such a good job of building negative reflexes into us that we often found ourselves overreacting when the least little thing went wrong. I found Glenn retreating into his books and ministry, rather than share his feelings. He didn't ignore the situation, but he kept his pain walled up inside a good deal of the time.

When we finally appeared before the juvenile court with Scott, it was obvious Scott wasn't going to get off so easily this time. On top of this, the attorney, who was collecting handsomely for appearing at our side, hadn't even read the court papers ahead of time. He made a rather lame opening statement, and it didn't take us long to realize that the judge was not impressed.

Scott was dressed neatly; he seemed to know how serious the charges were. When the judge mentioned the possibility of his spending the next two years in a boys' reformatory, both Scott's attorney and Glenn tried to reason with the judge, that the knife wasn't concealed but in Scott's hand—the judge dismissed that charge—and also that the amount of marijuana was so negligible that a beer would create a bigger "high." I could see the judge wasn't buying it; in fact, this line of reasoning just might increase Scott's sentence!

Finally I could stand it no longer. I had to speak up in that all-male courtroom. "Your Honor, I'm Scott's mother," I interrupted. "I just want to say that I'm *glad* Scott got caught. He deserves whatever you decide in this case."

Scott sucked in an audible breath. He probably saw any chance of freedom vanishing before his very eyes. He gave me a piercing look.

I ignored him and continued: "His father and I believe that going to a reformatory won't straighten Scott out. He has already made steps toward rehabilitating himself. About two weeks ago, he sought counseling and paid for it out of his own earnings. It was his idea, not ours. I ask you to keep this in mind." Having said what needed to be said, I sat down and folded my hands.

The judge cleared his throat. You could have heard a pin drop. "Is this true, young man?" he asked Scott.

"Yes, sir. I did go for counseling. I've been three times, and I think I can change, if I'm given the chance." He looked directly at the judge as he spoke. Scott knew his future was on the line, and for once he didn't blow it.

The judge studied all three of us for a long moment. "Well, young man, you can thank your lucky stars that your parents don't think you're beyond reform. If they're willing to put up with you, and you're willing to work with them, I'll release you to their custody and put you on probation until you're eighteen. If you mess up, you go to jail. And if you're seventeen or older and commit a crime, you can count on being certified as an adult and spending time in prison."

"I promise, your Honor—" Scott's voice cracked. "I will straighten up my act."

"Make sure you do." The judge pronounced his conditions for probation, and we left the courtroom to meet with Scott's new juvenile probation officer. Immediately I sensed that Scott wasn't going to have an easy time of it; this new probation officer acted as though he could hardly wait for Scott to mess up. However, Scott kept his composure during the interview, and we were soon free to leave.

"Wow, Mom!" he exclaimed. "You should have been a lawyer. You really saved my neck in that courtroom."

"No, I didn't, Scott," I said, tight-lipped, as we walked to the car. "You'd better recognize that the Lord Jesus Christ was in there, pleading your case. Nothing your father or I could have said would have changed things, if God didn't mean for you to have a second chance."

"Your mother is right, son." Glenn clapped a hand on Scott's shoulder. "Won't you turn your life over to Jesus? He can give your life meaning and purpose, and help you get your life straightened around."

"Cut the sermon, Dad," Scott retorted. "I believe in Jesus. I know He's in my heart. But I gotta do my own thing, okay?"

"Scott!" I cried, horrified by his glib callousness. "Stop this! Can't you see what you're doing to yourself? To us? We love you very much, yet you seem determined to ruin your life."

"Later, Mom," Scott cut me off. "I know I messed up, but things are going to be different now. I can change. You'll see."

Chapter 11. Broken Hearts, Broken Promises

Promises were quickly broken. Scott just didn't have it within him to make the necessary changes. It wasn't long before he was staying out late with his friends again. Then, to avoid getting picked up for violation of curfew, he would sneak back home in the early predawn hours.

Frequently he came home drunk and verbally abusive. On one occasion, he was on something stronger than marijuana or Jack Daniels; we wondered if it could be PCP, as during an argument with his sister, he picked her up bodily, one hundred and ten pounds dripping wet, and hurled her like a football across the living room.

He and Chris had frequent arguments, but being quick-witted, Chris usually managed to sidestep a fight. Scott, now nearly six feet tall, never tried to "muscle" me, but he did take on his Dad a couple of times in the backyard. Soon discovering he could "whup" his father, Scott was ecstatic. He called Glenn a "crazy old preacher man," ridiculing our Christian faith and gloating over our powerlessness to alter his behavior.

His probation officer kept in close touch, despite a heavy caseload. Despite our initial negative reaction to him, Glenn and I came to appreciate his efforts on Scott's behalf. We recognized Scott's ongoing struggle for independence, but also knew he needed restraint for his own good. His "P.O." was fortunately more reasonable than we were when Scott got arrested for joyriding at two-thirty one morning. We wanted his truck taken away permanently, but his probation officer intervened, pointing out that Scott needed transportation to meet one of the requirements of his probation—employment. By this time, our emotions were raw and it was hard for us to remain objective; the probation officer helped provide balance.

When Scott was seventeen, he was jumped by a teenage

gang, who clubbed him with metal pipes and tire chains. Friends found him and brought him home, where he soon regained consciousness on the couch.

I was about to call the police and an ambulance when Scott got to his feet shakily and began to pace, telling the world at the top of his lungs what he was going to do to the "punks" who had ganged up on him. His vile threats were more to impress his peers, I thought; besides, he was in no physical condition to carry out his threats.

Leaving Chris to keep an eye on him, I telephoned the police. By the time they arrived, Scott was nearly hysterical with pain. Wisely, they insisted we take Scott to the hospital and then come down to the station to file a report.

In the emergency room, Scott lay scowling up at the ceiling like a thundercloud. With his head packed in ice, he was wheeled off for back and chest x-rays. Blood in his urine indicated bleeding kidneys. His upper torso was covered with bruises and lacerations, where he had been kicked and beaten.

After a few hours, the ice reduced the facial swelling; we were relieved to see Scott's contorted features relax a bit. He had also stopped cursing and expressing a desire for revenge.

Once Scott was able to be discharged, we drove to the police station where he filed a report on the gang beating. Two weeks later, two gang members were arrested for battery with a deadly weapon. They each faced a twenty year sentence, but were allowed to plea bargain down to a gross misdemeanor and a $150 fine.

Scott was livid when he found out how the case had been handled. One of his friends had been pushed around by gang members, who threatened to burn down his family's house, because he had "fingered" the gang leader.

With the shoe on the other foot and Scott now the victim of a crime, we thought his response might be to appreciate how law-abiding citizens felt and mend his ways.

Such was not the case. Because justice was *not* meted out by the courts, Scott began to flaunt his hatred and contempt by yelling out obscenities at passing police cars. He swore he would personally get revenge on the gang members who had jumped him from behind. Whether he ever took the law into his own hands, I never found out. But he used every opportunity to vent his anger and resentment against anyone the least bit "pro-establishment."

This was a very scary individual in our midst, and it broke our hearts to see his rapid deterioration. We honestly didn't expect Scott, with his wild partying and the bad company he kept, to live to his twentieth birthday.

Over the next few months we had many tense, unproductive arguments with Scott over various behaviors of his. When he finally reached eighteen and his probation was lifted, we felt a sense of profound relief. Many of the rules that tempt minors to misbehave, such as drinking and breaking curfew, were no longer illegal. We hoped that Scott, now officially an adult, would settle into a saner period, instead of continuing to defy the restraints of society.

After wondering for some weeks if he should join the Armed Forces, Scott finally made his move. It was the worse possible decision he could have made.

One month past his eighteenth birthday, Scott went to Boise, and during that timeframe, a series of burglaries took place. Now an adult, he would have to face the consequences for his involvement. Excuses wouldn't hold water anymore. The grace period for minors had run out.

Chapter 12. Facing the Music

Scott was a nervous wreck as he prepared to return to Boise to stand trial. As he left to drive north with Glenn, he expressed relief that the waiting was over.

By pleading "nolo contendere," Scott hoped to avoid civil suit. He also hoped to circumvent a recommendation by his probation officer, who would probably have "roasted" him for what he had done. I doubt if I would have blamed his "P.O.," since he and all our family had tolerated more than enough of Scott's anti-social behaviors.

Glenn and I had come close to the breaking point on several occasions. During the last few months of Scott's probation as a juvenile, there were times when I found it impossible to stanch the flow of uncontrollable tears. A grief and a sadness welled up inside me that simply couldn't be stemmed. I knew without God's help, nothing could have kept me going. But because of Christ's love for sinners, including myself, I found the courage to believe some good purpose could emerge from the ashes of my love for Scott.

While Scott and Glenn were in Boise, I frequently prostrated myself before the Lord, pleading for Him to show our family mercy and provide strength.

When Glenn telephoned me after the sentencing, he was dumbfounded. "The judge flatly told Scott what a rotten person he was. He told him he didn't believe he was capable of being the 'brains' behind the burglaries, and after sentencing him to five years in prison—"

My temples began to throb, as I listened to Glen describe the trial. I was sure my heart would fail me. *Oh, please, God...*

"He sentenced Scott to five years in prison, Sandy," Glenn reiterated, yet he sounded strangely jubilant, as if a great weight had been lifted. "Then he turned around and placed Scott on probation for two years. If he keeps his act clean, he can have the felony conviction reduced to a misdemeanor. If he stays out of trouble for three years, he could have his record completely expunged."

Both of us knew Scott was good at maintaining minimal

compliance in order to avoid confinement. But the minute he completed a probationary period, he went right back to breaking the law. Even so, I sensed from Glenn's upbeat mood that God had again intervened. How strange. How unfailingly merciful our God is!

"I can't believe it!" I cried, and the tears and the adrenaline were flowing uncontrollably again. "You mean, Scott has been given another chance? Oh, Glenn—" I couldn't speak without choking up. In spite of all Scott had done, I still loved him; I still clung to the hope that he could be saved.

"Praise the Lord, Sandy. He hasn't let us down." Glenn's voice became choked with emotion, too. "I think it finally got through to Scott that his freedom was at stake, and there aren't going to be any more chances from here on out."

"Oh, Glenn, I do want Scott to stay out of trouble. After being on probation the past two years—" I shivered, afraid. I dreaded having to cope with Scott's continued rebellion.

"We're going to release Scott entirely to the Lord," Glenn told me, his voice gaining strength and resolve. "We'll be supportive, of course, but we won't try to rescue him or make excuses. If he messes up, that's his problem, not ours. He's an adult, and he either makes the grade on his own, or goes to jail. It's up to him."

"We'll just pray it all works out," I said, still not daring to hope too much. We had been through so much with Scott in the past that I was hesitant to share Glenn's enthusiasm. Somehow I sensed his hands-off approach was the only one that could possibly work.

"We'll be home late tomorrow. Love you, sweetheart," Glenn said and hung up.

The next afternoon Scott and Glenn stood on our doorstep. They had made the return trip in record time. Glen had the broadest smile on his face I'd seen in a long time. Scott looked more reticent; the strain showed in his face. He stood in the doorway, uncertain of my reaction.

Throwing my arms around him, I welcomed him as if nothing had happened. I knew he needed acceptance, regardless of the great wrong he had done. I didn't know what to say that might not sound judgmental or patronizing, so I avoided discussing the trial.

"Come on in! You two must be starved," I said chattily, ushering them in. "I've baked chocolate chip cookies—your favorites, Scott. And I've got everything laid out for a nice barbecue out back. How about something to eat?" I knew I was trying too hard. Scott must have felt it, too.

"I think I'd better wash up first, Mom," he said, quieter and more subdued than I'd seen him in a long time. "Boy, it's good to be home."

We embraced again wordlessly. He clung to me briefly, his cheek burning against the top of my head. Then he headed off to the shower, and Glenn and I were able to spend a moment together. It was such a comfort just to hold onto each other. Words were unnecessary. We each knew how the other felt.

A few minutes later, Shelley and Chris came home. They were relieved to learn that Scott was home. Over the past several years, we had seen the effect his behavior had had on their self-esteem, and we were pleased to see them rally around him now, as we prepared to barbecue hamburgers as a welcome home for our prodigal son.

Although there was much banter and Scott made a few joking remarks about the courtroom scene, nobody had any doubt that the trial had made an impact. It would remain seared in Scott's memory for a long time to come.

As our family laughed and talked together for the first time in months, Glenn and I winged a silent prayer to the Lord: *Please, God, help Scott make it this time.*

Chapter 13.
Tense Moments: Could Scott Make The Grade?

"Mom!" It was Chris on the phone. "Mom, Scott and I were just sitting here in the living room watching TV when the police came. They're here now, and they're hassling Scott something terrible. I think you'd better come home."

I was in my office, slogging my way through a pile of month-end reports when the call came. Suddenly every muscle in my body began to twitch. I felt powerless to hold myself together. My teeth even started chattering. I made a valid effort to get a grip on myself as I clutched the telephone receiver.

"Chris, I'm coming! Just keep calm."

I picked up my purse and dashed toward the door of my office. The new receptionist watched wide-eyed, as if I had just taken leave of my senses. In a way, I had.

"Where are you going, Mrs. Patterson?" she asked, dropping her pencils in surprise.

"Home. Cover for me, LeAn. I'll be back as soon as I can. Emergency." I was gone.

On the way home, I drove as fast as the speed limit allowed. My heart was pounding. I felt so shaky and upset that I was sure I would die of a heart attack right there behind the wheel. I had no idea what was going on at home, but Chris, our level-headed one, certainly sounded upset.

Screeching up to the front door of our home, I was surprised to find no police cars present. Leaping out, I was met by Chris and Scott, both highly agitated.

"What happened?" I walked inside and leaned against the living room wall to catch my breath.

"Oh, this nutty guy down the block got mad because my tires squealed as I came around the corner," Scott shrugged, trying to act nonchalant. "Anyway, these two cops came to the door, and they began giving me a bad time."

"That's right, Mom," Chris chimed in.

"I invited them in, and the next thing they're threatening to take us both in." Scott was certainly taking the situation better than I. My heart was still wobbling around in my chest.

"They left right after I telephoned you, Mom," Chris added. "I guess they didn't want any trouble from an adult."

"No, they just didn't want any witnesses," I said angrily and swung around to confront Scott. "You're *sure* you didn't do anything wrong?"

"I did zilch, Mom," he responded. "It's just because that guy down the block likes to hassle me." He noticed how upset I was and reached out a hand to steady me. "I'm sorry, Mom. I didn't know this would bother you so much."

"Bother!" I exclaimed, knowing I was not myself, but unable to stop my outburst. "Of course, I'm really upset! Don't do *anything* to make waves around here, Scott Patterson. *Please.*" I sat down and tried to collect myself.

Chris brought me a glass of water, which I accepted with a trembling hand. "Calm down, Mom. Everything's okay now."

"It's *not* okay." I took a sip. "I'm beginning to think this family is jinxed! How long is this sort of thing going to go on?"

"Take it easy, Mom." Scott seemed unnerved to see his mother, usually so "together," having hysterics. "Hey," he tried changing the subject, "I got a job today."

I sat up straight. "That's wonderful, Scott. Where?"

"Fixing machines at a health club. It isn't the greatest pay, just six dollars an hour, but I'll be able to start paying something back to you and Dad. I know it cost a lot for legal fees and traveling up to Boise." He looked apologetic.

"I don't care about the money, Scott. You know that. Just as long as you're working and happy." I set aside the water glass and stood up, smoothing my skirt. "Well, if the crisis is over, I should be getting back to work."

"As soon as I can, I plan to get my own place to live, so you and Dad can relax a little. Otherwise, every little thing that happens is likely to set you off." He smiled ruefully.

"You must think I'm a total nut," I said, smiling back. I ruffled his long hair and derived comfort from his quick hug. "Sorry I got so carried away."

Chris stood there. Suddenly I realized that all the concern and attention lavished on Scott must have made Chris feel left out in the cold.

"Chris, thanks for calling me," I said, giving him a hug. Then I picked up my purse and retrieved my car keys.

As I drove back to work, I realized how the office had become a haven from my problems at home. There was something to be said for predictable routine and "normalcy." I figured my job had probably kept me sane through all our recent troubles with Scott.

By the time I got to the office, I was actually humming a Gospel chorus I used to sing with my children when they were toddlers.

When Scott got his first paycheck two weeks later, he moved out. He moved just down the street to Ted's house. Although it meant an easing of tensions for us, my heart went out to Ted's mother. Scott had a voracious appetite, and I could just imagine him raiding her food pantry. He still came by the house every day for "snacks," as he termed his enormous Dagwood sandwich combinations.

Initially his truck cost nearly as much for repairs and gas as his salary brought in. There were also periods of unemployment, which didn't help. In a panic, I was tempted to help Scott by dipping into our personal savings, just so he wouldn't be tempted to steal. Sensing this wouldn't prevent Scott from getting involved in illegal activities, if he chose to go in that direction, I refrained from trying to rescue him. He had to take responsibility for himself.

After talking it over with Glenn, he and I did loan Scott a few dollars, which he paid back. We steered him to a part-time position as a janitor, in exchange for rent in an apartment complex. Although his finances were tight at first, as Scott gained experience, his employment record improved.

Meanwhile Scott and his girl friend Linda had their ups and downs, but it was clear she lent stability to his life. Her expectations of him were healthy ones, and although he sometimes complained about restrictions she placed on their relationship, he benefited. From their growing friendship, he was learning to be responsible to another person.

Joking but relieved, I told Glenn it was nice having Linda act as his unofficial probation officer, instead of us. I found it easier relating to Scott as an adult. He had always hated being treated as a child, and it felt good being able to put those days behind us.

Even though Scott reported weekly to the state probation and parole office, those really close to Scott did the most to reinforce his resolve to stay out of trouble.

One of the wonderful things we learned a few months after he was placed on probation was Scott's decision to eliminate drugs and alcohol from his life.

"I can't even carry on a decent conversation when I'm high, Mom," he told me one day while putting together a marathon ham sandwich. "Besides, Linda would get on my case if I did."

"I guess it's important to please her, isn't it?" Glenn remarked, putting down his newspaper.

"She's a royal pain sometimes, but I really love her. She understands my moods," he said, scraping mustard on his bread. "I'm the only person on the job who doesn't cap off the day with a six-pack of beer. The boss always buys soft drinks for me," he added between bites. "I'm one of his best workers, did you know that?"

"That's great, Scott," Chris chimed in. "You know something? You're making more money per hour than Mom!"

"Not bad for someone who hasn't finished high school," Scott gloated, washing everything down with a quart of milk. "Well, I gotta split. Linda expects me to pick her up from work. We're going shopping."

"See you later, dear," I called as he disappeared out the door.

Glenn vanished behind his newspaper again. From the smile on his face, I knew he was pleased with the way Scott was starting to handle life.

With Scott out of the house, we began to concentrate on getting Shelley through college. We were strapped financially, but she and Chris were doing so well in school that it was like a spiritual balm for Glenn's and my war-torn nerves. We still felt twinges of anxiety when we heard a police siren in the distance, or heard about another family whose child had gotten into trouble with the law. We felt special empathy for other parents' heartache, having lived through a succession of traumas with Scott.

After Scott began to settle down, he took the initiative to "bone up" and take the GED high school equivalency tests. Much to his relief and surprise, he passed! We were grateful that he now had an open door to pursue higher education, should he choose to pursue it.

Speeding tickets continued to plague Scott. He and Linda had tiffs and spats, but nothing serious enough to break them up. Scott was a delight to watch, as he wooed her with roses, candy, a new pair of jogging shoes, anything he thought she would enjoy. They gave every evidence of being in love.

Then one day Scott came over and threw himself into an easy chair. He had a dark scowl on his face. "That's it, Mom!"

he said with a savage gesture of his hand. "I've had it with Linda. She turned me down flat."

"What do you mean, Scott?" I asked, looking up from my mending.

"I actually asked her to marry me, and she said, 'No.' Can you beat that?" He looked up, his eyes watering.

"Maybe she feels it's too early to make a commitment," Glenn suggested in a neutral tone from his corner.

"Hey, if she doesn't know how she feels about me by now, she never will. I really love her," he added, rubbing his knuckles across his cheek. "But I'll be darned if I'm going to ask her again. Next time she'll have to ask—no, *beg*—me to marry her."

I had to smile. Here was Scott, now nineteen, wanting to settle down. I sympathized with him, but Linda also had a point. Scott still had over a year of probation left. He still had to prove himself worthy of her trust.

"Give it more time, Scott," I counseled. "Linda is a year older than you. She's smart not to get too deeply involved until your probation period is over."

"No, she just doesn't love me enough. And don't throw the past in my face!" He got up and began to pace. "I'm so tired of being reminded of that one lousy mistake I made—"

"Scott, whoa!" Glenn shot out of his chair and put a restraining hand on Scott's shoulder. "You've still got a lot of growing up to do, and so does Linda. Let's face it, what happened last year can't just be swept under the rug. It happened."

"That's the trouble with you and Mom. Always throwing things up to me." Scott shook off his father's hand and stared down at his shoes. "I feel so crummy when you ask me if I've seen my 'P.O.' and stuff."

"Scott, what really matters is getting your life straight with Christ. You've done a lot of changing—on the surface.

224

You've made some important decisions, and we're proud of you, son. But you haven't let Jesus be the Lord of your life."

"Lay off the religious bull!" Scott warned. His face was angry and flushed.

"I can't. I'm completely convinced that no matter how good things look outwardly, Scott, you'll never be able to handle disappointments and rejection, like right now, until you turn your life over to the Lord." Glenn looked Scott directly in the eye.

"Hey! Haven't I changed?" Scott countered defensively. "Get off my back, preacher man."

"Honey, Dad isn't trying to give you a bad time," I said. "We love you, and we're glad things are going better for you. But your father *is r*ight, you know."

"I asked Jesus in my heart a long time ago, Mom. I know he died for me. What more do you two want?" Scott threw his arms in the air and let them drop with a slap against his pant leg.

"It's not what *we* want. Scott, we're talking about the one decision that can change you on the inside. You need to surrender your life to Christ as *Lord*." Glenn's voice was firm as he faced his son.

Scott cleared his throat uncomfortably. "Why? You think maybe that will make Linda want to marry me? Haven't I changed enough for her? For you guys?" He seemed close to tears.

Glenn lowered his voice to a confidential tone. "Scott, what Linda decides is up to her. God isn't going to manipulate her, or you. He is only interested in your best interests."

"I wouldn't marry her now, even if she—" Scott began, sounding like a petulant little boy.

"Forget about that for a minute, Scott. God wants your heart, your mind, your strength, your total personality yielded to Him," Glenn persisted. "You'll never have a moment's peace until you let Him be Lord."

"No matter what you do, Scott," I said, smiling, "we're going to keep right on loving you. You might as well give up."

"You think I'm such a rotten sinner, don't you? Just because I messed up." Scott was getting more agitated.

"No worse than anyone else," Glenn said. "There aren't any 'better ' sinners than others, Scott. You should know that. But you *do* have a need deep inside, don't you, Scott? And only Christ can meet that need. Not even Linda can fill all your needs." Glenn hesitated, then took Scott into his arms the way he used to when Scott was a young child.

Suddenly Scott's head dropped against his father's shoulder, and his shoulders began to shake. He wept long and hard, filling the room with the sound of his sobs, until he seemed near collapse from the enormity of his sin and heartbreak. "How *can* you love me, Dad? I've done a lot more things than you and Mom know about. I'm no good. Nobody could love me—" His voice choked with a convulsive grief that revealed how deeply confused and full of self-loathing he had become.

"No, you are *loved*. You've always been loved." Glenn smoothed back the unruly hair from Scott's temple. I hadn't seen Glenn express such tenderness toward his son in many years. I sat with my hands in my lap, watching, but saying nothing. This moment belonged to them.

"But I've failed!" Scott stammered. "All my life I've failed....you...Mom. I never could get high grades like Shelley and Chris. I never could please my teachers..." He continued to heap condemnation on himself.

Gently Glenn placed his fingertips across Scott's lips. "Christ doesn't condemn you, Scott, so how can anyone else, including you?" He uttered those words with such a warmth of conviction that Scott stopped trying to contradict.

He stared at his father, new hope slowly dawning in his

226

eyes. "Christ...truly *loves*...me?" He spoke as if testing the words, almost not daring to believe it.

Glenn nodded. The tears were streaming down his cheeks, but a light shone in his eyes, communicating a father's love for his son.

"I've been such a meathead! How *could* I have been so blind!" Scott said, still struggling to shake off his damaged self-perception. "Jesus loves *me*! It's not just a nice little nursery rhyme, is it? It's *real*! Why didn't I ever understand that before?" He almost whooped with joy, as he looked first at his father and then across the room at me. "Jesus loves *me*! That's where it's really at, isn't it?"

"It's not so hard to turn your life over to Someone who loves you that much, now is it, Scott?" Glenn's voice was gently persuasive.

"That's what I gotta do right now, Dad."

They prayed together on their knees, and God met Scott in a glorious way. From that moment on, Scott was a new man in Christ.

Epilogue

Even after Scott's life-changing experience, he still experienced frustrations on the job, knew periods of unemployment, and had problems in his relationship with Linda. What *was* different was the way he handled life. He felt differently about himself inside. He knew he was truly forgiven of the past—by the Lord and by us.

Before long, he began finding ways to encourage others who were struggling with similar burdens. He stopped thinking only of himself, his needs and wants. He began showing more kindness to Shelley. He began to communicate and share with Chris, who quietly idolized his older brother for his physical prowess, in ways that had never been possible before.

And after years of straining to love Scott "in spite of" his behaviors, Glenn and I were finally able to enjoy his interaction with us. We still continue to support and uphold each other. We thrash out misunderstandings and problems as they arise. But the level of caring has changed. Often we find ourselves on the receiving end of Scott's love, something that hadn't happened in years.

Scott successfully completed his two years' probation, had his felony conviction reduced to a misdemeanor, and later had his criminal records expunged. That day came one month after he and Linda exchanged vows at the altar in the church we served.

Today he and Linda have three adorable little girls and belong to a church that has an active men's fellowship that spends time reaching out to troubled teenagers. He owns his own business, designing physical fitness workouts for busy executives.

Four years after Scott stood trial, Shelley confided to us one of the traumatic reasons for his teenage rebellion: While he was held in detention at age thirteen, Scott had witnessed the rape of an eleven-year-old boy by two older teenagers. That young boy's cries for help went unheeded. Small-framed himself at the time, Scott was powerless to come to the boy's aid. Vicariously, he suffered the shame and degradation of that helpless eleven-year-old. Everyone in that cell stood rooted to the spot, watching.

Why any eleven-year-old was placed in such danger will probably never be answered. Where he is today may be a direct result of what happened to him that terrible night.

I cannot help that boy, except to pray for him. I do know, however, what the experience did to our Scott. He came home resolved never again to trust adults. Had not his own parents— however well meaning—placed him in that hole to "teach him a lesson"? In his eyes, we had abandoned him and exposed him to personal danger. The lesson he came away with that night nearly destroyed his life—and his very soul.

From then until his conversion, Scott's attitude toward teachers, parents, and authority figures in his life was one of hatred and defiance. He ran wild, afraid to trust, to love, or to let anyone love him. It took many years before we understood what had happened to destroy Scott's ability to exercise faith and make appropriate decisions for his life.

There are so many things we parents don't know about our own children. We can't possibly know all the things that influence them. We just see them out of control, hurting themselves and those around them. But even when our emotions are rubbed raw and we experience "burn out" from the continual struggle, we can't give up.

For were not these the children entrusted to us by God? Are they not primarily *our* responsibility?

Our marriage vows, "For better, for worse," surely ought to apply to our children as well. Marriage and children are both part of the same commitment, intended to bring the entire family together and preserve it as a whole.

We need to ask ourselves: How are we choosing to deal with our pain—and theirs? Are we willing to be teachable? To love regardless of the cost to us personally? These are among the many agonizing questions we must ponder as families. The answers are *never* found without much soul-searching.

Oh, you say, *I've turned the other cheek and walked more second miles than I can recall—and all for what? I don't think I care anymore.*

My answer to you is: You must not stop loving! For who will, if you don't? It will take faith. It will take all the love that is in you, and *more*—so much more: **It will take Christ's love working in and through you.** It will take tenacity and stamina. But you can do it. Not in your own strength, but in the strength of Christ, who "ever liveth to make intercession for you." [Hebrews 7:35]

There were times when our family could have given up. But His indwelling Holy Spirit made the difference between defeat and victory, between dwelling on the crucifixion side of our heartache and the resurrection side of our faith.

Today I am convinced that if we, as Scott's family, had given up on him—if we had washed our hands of him and turned our backs—our son would be in an institution today.

He probably would never have found his way back, or become an asset to society. It's also doubtful he would ever have accepted Jesus Christ as both his Savior *and* his Lord.

I wish I could say that all similar stories have a happy ending. My heart aches over the unneccessary carnage in our streets, as many of our young people lose their lives through senseless violence. Especially I sorrow for the parents left behind to grieve. Our own son could easily have become another statistic. For those of you who have lost a son or a daughter because of their involvement in drugs, I pray for you.

I also urge you to translate the love you have for your child into some positive action, so that the spread of this terrible pestilence can be stopped.

We must do battle on our knees, and we must get involved in our communities.

It is hard waiting for God to answer prayers. Sometimes it seems to us as heartbroken parents that God has turned His back. *This is simply not true!*

I want to reassure anyone who is tempted to feel abandoned or despairing: *God does care.* He has not finished His work in *any* of us.

That's why the Lord invites us:

"Come to Me, all who are weary and burdened down, and I will give you rest. Take my yoke upon you and learn from me, for I am gentle and humble of heart, and you will find rest for your souls. For my yoke is easy, and my burden

is light." [Matthew 11:28-30]

I would *never* presume to tell other agonizing parents what the answer is to their individual dilemma. But from the bottom of my heart, I wish to stress that, as parents, we must continue to demonstrate the true spirit of Christian love and acceptance.

Ask yourself: *Is there any end to God's love for me? Then, what should my response to His unceasing love be?*

Scripture commands us to be "imitators of Christ." *Never stop loving!* Don't stop caring for the lost, be they your own or someone else's children. **Our attitude may mean the difference between heaven and hell to a young person struggling to make it through those crucial formative years.**

We are engaged in a spiritual warfare for the minds and hearts of our children. As parents, we have been given a holy task and a high calling. Let us, therefore, love them even when they are unlovely and unlovable, believing always that the same God who loved *us* enough to send His Son to die for our sins, also loves our children with "an everlasting love."

Even when your heart is breaking, don't panic.

Remember, Christ is still in control. There is nothing too hard for Him to accomplish. Your faith *will* be rewarded, and God *will* reveal His will to you, step by step. He has given you the **power to choose**—to love, to believe, to overcome.

Our family walked through the fire. We survived it.

You can, too!

Even though your walk may be totally diffferent.

All any of us have to do is *live* it, one day at a time...

In the power of God, and relying constantly on the saving grace of Christ, for...

"With God, all things are possible."
[Matthew 19:26; Mark 10:27]

The Power of Kingdom Living

by

John Dan, M.A., M.Div.

"Thy Will Be Done on Earth,
as It Is in Heaven."
[Matthew 6:10; Luke 11:2]

Chapter 11.
Power Living on The Gospel Road

Kingdom living is dependent upon our response to four basic components that work together to help us access the spiritual riches available to us in Christ:

1. **The Motivator: Our Pain**. Life's journey brings us into experiences that demonstrate the limitations and the true state of our human condition, our sin and alienation. One does not need to be a Christian to realize this. Pain and cost startle us out of complacency, forcing us to recognize our vulnerabilities and how great our spiritual and other needs really are. At this stage, we either become teachable and choose the way of healing, or we seek escape through various cover-up activities. In our search to alleviate life's pain, we exercise our power to choose. The decision we make in our spiritual quest—because that's exactly what it is—is *crucial* to our future success and wellbeing.

2. **The Cross: Our Salvation**. Jesus Christ, the Son of God, walked this earth as one of us. He literally became the "visible expression of the invisible God." [*cf.* Colossians 1:15-16] This is such a radical idea, that only God could conceive of it!

The disciple John begins his Gospel and his first epistle with this recognition [John 1:1-5 and I John 1:1-3]. Jesus becoming a part of the human scene, in a temporal, vulnerable body like ours, shows the lengths to which God was willing to go to rescue us, His creation.

His compassion and wisdom, His readiness to heal and deliver us from First Order system thinking were demonstrated over and over in the Gospels and other Biblical writings. That this was God's plan from the beginning is evident in prophetic writings and foreshadowings throughout the Old Testament. The sacrificed Lamb of God [Exodus], the suffering Servant marred beyond recognition [Isaiah 53] and many more pictures of the Savior's mission to His people have been the subject of many excellent exegetical studies.

Jesus' was executed like a common criminal for *our* sins, *our* transgressions. His sacrifice on the Cross to obtain our deliverance is the focal point of God's message to us in holy Scripture. "Neither is there salvation in any other: for there is no other Name under heaven given among men whereby we *must* be saved." [Acts 4:12]

Jesus Christ's death on the Cross acquits us of our sin, absorbs our sinful condition unto Himself, and sets us free from our bondage. By faith, we can appropriate His grace and His power to live a new life. His resurrection on the third day is God's guarantee that He has conquered the last enemy we face, *i.e.*, death. As we respond to His sacrifice on the Cross and allow His life to be lived in us, we discover that he has also conquered every other enemy, or tyranny, that has held us in its control.

Our liberation and our futures depend on our response to God's generosity. He gave His only Son, Jesus, so that we might "not perish but have everlasting life." [John 3:16-17] This "everlasting life" is not just life beyond the grave; it begins from the moment you receive Jesus as your Savior and Lord, and it means quality living, starting right here and now.

3. **The Comforter: The Holy Spirit's Role**. In His astounding generosity and compassion, God sends the Holy Spirit to minister to our hearts. The work of the Holy Spirit is essential to our salvation. He convicts and guides us out of the treacherous broad ways of life. We become born again because He comes into our spirit, making us a child of the King of the Universe, our Creator. We lose our status as blind

slaves to sin and the mindset that seeks to destroy and hold us in bondage to darkness and fear. Once we open our hearts to the truth of the Gospel, He never leaves us. His work in our lives is an on-going process. He brings about our transformation by implanting and restoring the Image of God within us. He becomes our constant Source of comfort and our strength. We can rely on Him without reservation.

4. **The Power: God's Deliverance**. Our choosing God releases His power in our lives. This is not a one-time infusion of His power, but an on-going process, as He reveals to us our vulnerabilities and continually provides a way of deliverance. [I Corinthians 10:13] As Paul reminds us in II Corinthians 1:10, "[Christ] *delivered* us from so great a death, and *does* deliver: in [Him] we trust that He *will* yet deliver us." In other words, the work of deliverance takes place—past tense, present tense, and future tense.

Clearly, once God has begun a work in us, He continues to rescue us from the "old nature" which tries to reassert itself and reclaim what it has lost, *i.e.*, us! Scripture describes this vigilance on God's part as a continual "hovering" of the Holy Spirit, Who intercedes on our behalf. [Romans 8:26, 27, 34] Christ Jesus Himself also continually intercedes before the Father's throne. [Hebrews 7:25]

We are never left without access to God's mercy and grace. We are surrounded by His presence. All we need to do is ask, seek and knock. [Matthew 7:7]

In the first four sections of this book, we explored what it means to exercise the power to choose. We examined a number of tyrannies that militate against the human spirit and keep us from dealing effectively with life. We took a look at the freedoms we have in Christ to overcome the flesh. Over and over, we have emphasized the fact that our *only* defense is found in God: "Not by might, nor by power, but by My Spirit, saith the Lord of hosts." [Zechariah 4:6]

Jesus warned that trying to hang onto false security—to "save" our life—was the surest way to lose it. [Matthew 16:25; Mark 8:35; Luke 9:24; 17:33] He urges His disciples, instead, to "take up your cross and follow me." [Matthew 16:24; Mark 8:34; 10:21; Luke 9:23; and a number of passages in John's Gospel, including 10:27, 12:26 and 21:22]

Do not waste time chafing over the fact that you have been given a cross to bear. Just get on with it. Tough as it may seem, get that shoulder under the burden, take a deep breath, knowing His strength will never fail you, and—*heave!* (Remember, a stronger shoulder than ours is there to do the actual lifting.)

As a former merchant marine cadet at Kings Point, New York, I have spent a fair amount of time on nineteenth century sailing vessels. If you have ever watched a handful of sailors raise thousands of pounds of canvas sail to the top of a mast, or haul anchor cable, you know it takes a combination of team-work and a brisk chanty to overcome the limitations of the flesh.

Imagine yourself as a crew member and Jesus as the Boatswain. He not only calls the chant, but provides the muscle to raise the sagging sail of your faith, so that it can catch the powerful wind of God's Spirit and carry you safely through the rough seas of life.

Remember, "All things are possible with God." [Matthew 19:26] Claim that promise! Whatever trials or trauma you face, God's resources are yours through faith in Jesus Christ.

During the Vietnam War, a number of American pilots and crews were shot down over enemy territory. They were captured and became "guests" of the Hanoi Hilton and similar resorts. In these human pits of despair and degradation, these men were subjected to torture, interrogation, isolation, starva-tion, physical neglect, and unhygienic conditions. Every attempt was made to break them down psychologically, emotionally and physically. Their captors did everything possible to demoralize and break these men's spirits.

Many succumbed to disease, discouragement and death. Their heroic last days may never be revealed, but they didn't make it out alive. Even so, we must not grieve as those who have no hope. Those who *did* make it out relate stories that should make us proud of all our servicemen, the ones who survived and those who have gone on to a better reward.

Amazingly, many men hung on, their spirits unbroken. They dug deep into their spiritual roots and discovered the power that enabled them to survive. By *faith*, they outwitted and overcame the spiritual siege being waged against them.

They also recognized the existence of an even greater enemy within and refused to give in to it. This enemy's Biblical name is Legion: These men came to know it well, especially during the first weeks and months of their captivity. It is *fear*. An insidious betrayer of the human spirit, fear seeks to win over rational thinking and faith by whittling away at one's belief system. Allowed to run rampant, it will strip away hope and suck the very marrow out of life.

Basically, these airmen faced a choice: Choose the weapons of the spirit and live, or choose to listen to their fears and die. Given such a choice, what would you do? Fight the good fight, or give up? Give the enemy the satisfaction of having beaten you, or, as the apostle Paul put it, 'stand against the wiles of the devil." [Ephesians 6:1]

Paul certainly knew what these airmen were up against. He spent years in Romans dungeons, in the stinking holds of rat-infested ships, and on forced marches through hostile open country. He slept on the ground in inclement weather, suffered deprivation of all kinds. This only strengthened his determination to preach the Gospel! And to see those who were captive to sin set free. As his letters attest, **his sufferings only sharpened his spiritual understanding**.

Like Dietrich Bonhoeffer, executed by the Nazis during World War II, and Watchman Nee, imprisoned for years in Communist China, Paul saw two enemy camps, God's and Satan's, set in opposition: *"We wrestle not against flesh and blood, but against principalities, against powers, against the rulers of the darkness of this world, against spiritual wickedness in high places."* [Ephesians 6:12]

Millions have paid the ultimate price with their lives. But with the promise of an "unending life" in Christ, the threat of persecution loses much of its power. The spirit is *always* stronger than the flesh and will win out.

When evil occurs, in most cases, the perpetrator is merely the servant of sin. On one level, he/she certainly *does* mean to commit grievous harm. The Bible speaks about being "the servant of sin." Our only way of escape is through Christ. Those who reject Christ automatically become locked into adversarial relationships.

Many Christians encounter persecution in one form or another, either because of their faith, or out of envy. You may have encountered it yourself—on the job, from a neighbor or even a carnal Christian. Without ever intending to call attention to yourself, you may have found yourself the target of someone's personal vendetta. If this happens, there isn't much you can do about it, except to place your faith in operation and take a stand "against all the fiery darts of the wicked." [Ephesians 6:16] Immerse yourself in the Word of God. Pray for God's protection and also for the person(s) coming against you.

Above all, remember that you cannot hide the Light you have received from the Lord. Some may resent or mistake your patience and forbearance for weakness, but continue to maintain a stand against all manifestations of evil, but do so in a spirit of love. In doing so, you will "heap coals of fire on his head. Be not overcome by evil, but overcome evil with good."

[Romans 12:20b-21]

My friend Doris experienced unrelenting persecution for several months from a resentful colleague after she received a grant in recognition for her accomplishments as an educator. Instantly she became the target of harassing phone calls, vile threats, stalking, libel and slander. Finally, the stress became too much, and she was hospitalized. All along, she had sensed great satanic activity, but had been powerless to stop it.

Lying there in the hospital, Doris had to choose: How was she going to ward off the oppressive effects of this man's vicious and unwarranted attacks against her? Was she going to operate in the flesh, or in the power of God? It was not a difficult decision. She relinquished the battle to God.

Gradually, drawing heavily upon God's Word for strength, wisdom and guidance, Doris began to pull out of the oppression of the enemy. She had to accept the fact that this man's hate-smear campaign emanated out of envy and greed. In time, she came to regard her colleague's actions as symptoms of a deep spiritual sickness. She began to pray for his salvation. She was able to find forgiveness in her heart for this man when she recognized how needy he was spiritually.

In a matter of weeks, she was well again. Doris later wrote, "Believe me, when your good name and career are on the line, and someone is willfully, maliciously trying to ruin you—possibly even do you physical harm—a Christian has no better defense than the Word of God. Hallelujah, what a Savior!"

Persecution arising out of envy, strife, or any number of human failings is difficult to deal with. We are in a spiritual battle. When we place the individual who is causing us so much grief in God's hands, we are already on the way toward inner peace and healing. We cannot change how others regard us, or what they say or do. We can only choose how we respond.

Heaping "coals of fire" on them by loving acts may free us emotionally and spiritually. There are times when this is appropriate and very effective. Sometimes, you just have to ignore the perpetrator and move on, resolutely at first and later with greater ease as you distance yourself.

The Tyranny of Political Correctness
vs. the Freedom to Think, Assess and Act.

Being able to think for ourselves is tremendously freeing. Even though we examined the tyranny of conformity in Chapter 3, it seems appropriate to examine where this can lead, when pushed to the outer limits, as is happening more and more often in recent history.

Today there are many high priests and priestesses of the "politically correct" movement trying to push their doctrine down everyone else's throats. They contend that no one should ever be offended or upset by having to listen to opposing views; *i.e.*, it is unacceptable to harbor ideas and opinions that are at variance with what the elite, or controlling, group considers proper.

These "thought police" reject any term, opinion, or idea, however lightly made, that doesn't fall in line with the "politically correct" party line. The media and so-called intelligentsia of this country have pursued this line of reasoning to absurd lengths, coercing and exacting compliance through expulsion, ridicule, "social consciousness" classes, and various threats that cover a whole range of monetary, academic, career and social punishments. Their tactics are not unlike those employed during the McCarthy hearings, only this time the fear and hate mongers are pushing a liberal agenda.

Of course, it is the height of hypocrisy and arrogance for any group to presume to dictate how the rest of us should think or what opinions we should be allowed to express. This type activity can only take place when those involved are locked into First Order System thinking, be they in government, religion, business, education, or other special interest groups. [*Cf.*, **Power to Change**.]

Those of us who prefer to think for ourselves see significant parallels and warning signs as to what the future holds in store. We also treasure our **power to choose** as an integral part of our spiritual heritage.

Inherent in the exercise of choice is risk, the risk of offending and being offended. Failing to see the underlying menace of such attempts at people control, many people give up their freedom to make decisions and take action that will benefit them, out of fear that choosing may "offend" or stir up others against them.

Conformity limits our power to choose and act on the major issues that effect our lives. The view that *somehow I must be a bad person if others are hurt or offended by what I say or do*, shuts down thinking, learning ability, personal growth and creative interaction.

Unfortunately, this distorted view is fast becoming the pervasive "norm" at every level of our social structure. This germ can only reproduce more active evil.

There is a big difference between someone being deliberately offensive in order to devalue others, and someone who is offended because someone else acts out of responsible self-interest and conviction.

Suppose you or I make a decision to purchase an article of clothing, or take some other action that someone else finds offensive or disagreeable. The problem lies within the person who feels offended, not you or me. You and I have not made a deliberate decision to cause offense; our choice was based upon a totally different set of criteria. If others are offended, it is because they *choose* to be offended.

To be governed by the fear of giving offense is a sure way to get the life squeezed out of the human spirit.

Playing it safe inhibits people from taking creative and

necessary risks in life. Playing it safe in the face of any evil or tyranny only propagates and allows evil to become more deeply entrenched.

A New Perspective of Life's Journey

Fortunately faith frees us to recognize distorted thinking and the mind-manipulating tactics so often employed to immobilize people caught up in not going against the "norm."

During World War II, over 75,000 Jews were deported from France and put to death in Nazi gas chambers. Members of the French Resistance, many of them Christians, suffered a similar fate for their "offense" against the powerful Third Reich.

Yet the humble farming community of Le Chambon-sur-Lignon ignored the danger to themselves when they were ordered to register and turn over to the German occupational forces every Jew living in their area.

In direct disobedience to Hitler's henchmen, they opened their homes to thousands of fleeing Jewish refugees. They fed and hid them, supplied them with fake passports, and sent them on their way in safety. Hundreds of Jewish children were boarded and educated in their village throughout the war.

Among these children was a baby born in Le Chambon, Pierre Sauvage, who later returned to the area to investigate his roots and the extraordinary events that had taken place.

In his documentary, *"Weapons of the Spirit,"* Pierre Sauvage lauded these people for saving over 5,000 Jews from extermination and for making a "contribution toward the reconstruction of the world."

He recognized that these descendants of simple French Huguenot stock were no strangers to persecution themselves, and so it was not surprising that their hearts went out to these Jews fleeing their homeland. Their efforts to rescue Jews were based *solely* upon a faith that was solidly anchored in the Word of God. So contagious was their spirit that even the German commandant in Le Chambon got caught up in their "conspiracy of goodness" and looked the other way!

Yet, when interviewed, these Christian farmers expressed surprise that anyone thought they had done anything remarkable. One old lady, who had taken in the Sauvage family, explained: "Jesus told us to feed the hungry and take care of the sick. We just did what Jesus told us to do."

These people simply did what they felt had to be done to resist evil. They harbored no fear or hatred in their hearts, only love. Even when the village church was surrounded by German troops and their pastor was arrested, they went on smuggling Jews past the noses of the Nazis!

During an interview by Bill Moyer on PBS-TV, Pierre Sauvage pointed out that the Holocaust could never have occurred, were it not for the apathy of Christians, both in Europe and in the United States.

Both Moyer and Sauvage also agreed that any community was capable of doing what the farmers of Le Chambon did. Very ordinary people do extraordinary things when (1) they are spiritually healthy, and (2) the opportunity presents itself for them to do good to fellow travelers who come across their path.

As a therapist, I found it especially noteworthy that when Pierre Sauvage showed his film, *"Weapons of the Spirit,"* at a gathering of the American Psychiatric Association, these simple French peasants received a standing ovation.

Their mental, spiritual and emotional health made otherwise ordinary lives powerful. This power was translated into action. What made them radiant with health was the way they lived out their faith, empowered by our Lord's injunction, *"Thy will be done on earth, as it is in heaven."* [Matthew 6:10; Luke 11:2

The next time we are tempted to despair because of the encroachment of evil in our world, we should remember what the collective faith of Le Chambon's Christian community accomplished. The sovereignty of God ruled in their hearts, endowing them with spiritual power and an unshakable inner peace, despite great political pressures and personal danger.

It's interesting to note that while these people quietly set about rescuing Jews, intellectuals all over Europe wrung their hands in helplessness, agonizing over the encroachment of evil and the Nazis' "inhumanity to their fellow men." Hitler himself was assisted in carrying out his heinous crimes by a brilliant staff, many of them Ph.Ds. Obviously education was not to be the salvation of Europe.

Pierre Sauvage made an astute observation about what makes for powerful living: "People who agonize don't act; people who act don't agonize."

The peasant farmers of Le Chambon didn't even lock their doors against the Nazis at night! They slept soundly, because their conscience was clear and Christ was their peace.

Each of us is individually responsible to God for the decisions and choices we make. We *are* our brother's keeper. There may come a time when we may be called upon to stand between someone else and great harm.

In our human vulnerability, this may seem an impossibility. But trusting the sovereignty of God to see you along the darkened trail ahead, you may be surprised how many candles you leave lit behind you, and what God may be pleased to accomplish through you.

Who knows? Your experience may have brought you, like Queen Esther, to the "kingdom for such a time as this." [Esther 4:16] When you encounter tyranny and oppression that binds, either within yourself or others, break its hold. Claim God's victory. And remember to lift that lantern of faith high, so that others may see to cross over and join you.

But we're running ahead of ourselves on the narrow Gospel road, aren't we?. We need not concern ourselves with what God may choose to do through us. Our job is to be about the business of living, knowing that in Him are found all the inner resources to face today and tomorrow without fear.

Operating from a position of power is the result of right choosing. Not only is it helpful to recognize the destructive patterns at work in our own lives and in those around us, but we must ask God to work within, transforming and empowering us daily.

Working through personal problems and crises becomes easier when we realize that we are not alone and that "power belongs to the Lord," Who is not slow to respond. [Psalm 62:11]

As we commit to Him all that we hold most dear in this world, Paul's certainty can be ours: "He is able to keep that which I have committed unto Him against that day." [II Timothy 1:12] What better place to commit our "treasure" than into God's hands?

No matter how dark the path, or what the obstacles are, your traveling Companion Jesus will show you the way.

Remember, long before creation, Jesus chose you to be His. So now—this day, if you've never done so—choose Jesus to be your Lord.

For when you choose to trust Him, He gives you power to live.

"You are God's, and you have overcome: because greater is He that is in you, than he that is in the world."
[I John 4:4]

THE END.

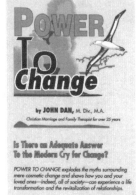

Words of Praise for POWER TO CHANGE:

POWER TO CHANGE... "addresses what I see to be the very heart of our national dilemma...which, I believe, derives from our abandonment of God in our thinking. God bless you, brother."
> --**Dr. Richard C. Halverson**,
> Chaplain, United States Senate

"It is a joy for me to recommend **POWER TO CHANGE**...a book that reflects many years of research and practical ministry... I strongly believe it will find a wide market among Christian workers who are interested in mental, spiritual and social wholeness, and will also make a valuable contribution to evangelism."
> --**Dr. Bill Thomas**, Associate Evangelist,
> Luis Palau Evangelistic Association.

'**POWER TO CHANGE** must have a great market in the field of psychology and psychiatry. The thrilling part of the book is the fact that Jesus, *only*, affects the power to change in our lives."
> --**Dale Evans Rogers**, Christian Author.

"John Dan writes about change...not just rearranging the chairs, but change with substance and at the spiritual core of our being... This book can create possibilities for you."
> --**Rev. Jerome Blankenship,**
> United Methodist Clergy; Reviewer for
> *Christian Century* and *Circuit Rider*.

"I highly recommend this book to counselors and pastors alike."
> --**Rev. Kenneth Kliever**, Region Minister,
> American Baptist Churches of Arizona.

"**POWER TO CHANGE** could be used effectively in both academic and pastoral settings...in both sermon preparation and adult educational classes...in Pastoral Counseling courses at theological seminaries... Personal transformation is what many aspire to, and **POWER TO CHANGE** explains how to achieve it."
> --**Dr. Francine Green, Director,** Social Services,
> Division of Mental Health and Mental Retardation
> Southern Nevada Adult Mental Health Services;
> also an Ordained Methodist Clergywoman.